THE GREAT RETURN,
THAT UNLIMITED POWER

THE GREAT RETURN,
THAT UNLIMITED POWER

T.B. ELLIS

XULON PRESS

Xulon Press
2301 Lucien Way #415
Maitland, FL 32751
407.339.4217
www.xulonpress.com

Unless otherwise indicated, Scripture quotations taken from the King
James Version (KJV) – *public domain*.

Scripture quotations taken from the New American Standard Bible
(NASB). Copyright © 1960, 1962, 1963, 1968, 1971, 1972, 1973,
1975, 1977, 1995 by The Lockman Foundation. Used by permission.
All rights reserved.

Paperback ISBN-13: 978-1-6628-1512-6

Hard Cover ISBN-13: 978-1-6628-1513-3

Ebook ISBN-13: 978-1-6628-1514-0

FOR THOSE AFFECTED BY...
OPIOIDS, A MENTAL HEALTH CONCERN
OR KNOW SOMEONE LIKE THAT,
OR DEPRESSION...

This book is dedicated to:
my beloved children
my beloved grandchildren
my extended family and friends
and you.

Hast thou not known? Hast thou not heard, that the ever-lasting God, the Lord, the Creator of the ends of the earth fainteth not, neither is weary? There is no searching of his understanding. He giveth power to the faint; and to them that have no might he increaseth strength. Even the youths shall faint and be weary, and the young men shall utterly fall: But they that wait upon the Lord shall renew their strength...

Isaiah 40: 28-31
King James Version

Table of Contents

Preface | xiii

CHAPTER 1
Unraveling | 1

CHAPTER 2
Pressing Forward: Drugs, Side Effects,
And Related Divergences | 5

CHAPTER 3
We Are Products Of Our Past | 17

CHAPTER 4
Up And Becoming | 37

CHAPTER 5
Unlocking The Code | 57

CHAPTER 6
Sour Grapes | 61

CHAPTER 7
Getting A Good College Education At NCC | 65

CHAPTER 8
The Unknown And A Carefree Spirit (Laval) | 75

CHAPTER 9
The Sit-Ins | 81

CHAPTER 10
First Job: French Teacher AND Purdue Student | 87

CHAPTER 11
Warming the Heart | 93

CHAPTER 12
Head of Household | 111

CHAPTER 13
My Theory | 119

ADDENDUM
Southern Family History | 125

Afterword | 129

Acknowledgments | 131

Abbreviations | 137

Notes | 139

Preface

THE INITIATIVE FOR WRITING THIS BOOK IS A quest to find out what caused me to go out of my head, to lose control of thinking and reality one day while hospitalized at age twenty-six. Before this, I had never taken much more than vitamins or an occasional Bufferin if I had a complaint. But things changed after becoming a patient in the mental health system, and it would prove to be a rather far-reaching endeavor. The doctors said that they didn't know the cause of this sudden, unexpected, and unexplained traumatic event which I now call my *self* in shambles. I'd never heard the names of many of the drugs that would be prescribed, nor experienced many of the side effects that followed.

Afterward, I was always concerned about maintaining that sense of my core *self*. This was my first time consciously singling out the *self* as another part of me that could be damaged just like any other part of my body. "For as the body is one, and hath many members, and all the members of that one body, being many, are one body: so also is Christ... And whether one member suffers, all the members suffer with it..." (1 Cor. 12: 12-26). Thus, the trek to find a clue that could have foreshadowed or contributed to this unfortunate event began. I hope my quest will also benefit you.

Chapter 1

Unraveling

NO ONE WAS STIRRING IN THE HALLWAY. IT was eerily quiet, and then something stirred inside me. *Where am I?* The room was kind of dark and painted brown with bars on the windows. You couldn't see outside. *Where is this? What am I doing here? How did I get here?* I wondered. A flashback of an old lady sitting in a rocking chair jolted me slightly. *How long have I been here? Am I senile?* Although still quite confused, this flashback indicated some change in my spirit. I remembered seeing this old lady when I went home one weekend with a friend from college, and this calmed my feelings a bit. At least the memory of my college friend, Gus, indicated that my mind was still active.

After a moment, a mellow voice from across the room chimed, "Hi." The voice was soft enough not to startle me. My eyes shifted and locked on a dark-complexioned lady sitting in a chair. "What's your name?" she asked. "I've been waiting for you to wake up." I uttered my name feeling quite relieved that I knew my name. This was reassuring as I realized my mind wasn't a blank slate. Feeling quite pleased, I was little by little regaining a sense of *self.* The bed restraint was in view, but I can't recall when, how, or who released me from it. Had I been thrashing about uncontrollably? I wondered what happened, but I didn't ask.

Moving along, the dark-complexioned lady who I assumed was a nurse, led me out of the room into the hallway. The idea of surgery, bandages, a baby girl, and a husband were just facts floating somewhere out there in the cosmos with no place to land. I had lost some time, or maybe even days, just like being hit on the head and left unconscious. It came to mind that I might never know what happened in that interim.

Then shortly, the dark-complexioned lady said, "Let's go down the hall." She showed me to a room and told me, "This is your roommate." The lady didn't speak but just kept gazing up at the ceiling. Soon it was time to eat, but I realized I couldn't carry my food tray. It dawned on me that the restraint had injured my back; it didn't take much thinking for me to realize what had happened.

Before long, the doctor came and prescribed an Anacin and Bufferin for my back. As the conversation ensued, I asked questions and he told me that I had a setback. He used the analogy of breaking a leg to compare my going out of my head. "No matter what caused the leg to break, everyone has to go through certain procedures to heal." He told me this to convince me that I needed this kind of treatment.

I had been transferred from the maternity ward to the psychiatric ward and would have to stay there for two weeks. But little by little, things leading up to this point began to resurface. For two days after the C-section, I could not sleep, but couldn't reason well enough to realize I needed to tell someone. Then on the third morning, I was just very tired and felt all keyed up, just wanting to go to sleep. But my roommate, Rita, was continuously talking on the phone, exactly what I didn't need. Then, to my amazement, her voice began to speed up, faster, and faster and faster; she sounded like one of those old school tape recorders on fast forward just squeaking as the tape on the reel was about to run out, like when I was teaching French. Only there was no French dialog, "Bonjour, mademoiselle, comment allez vous?" Slowly, but surely, I realized I was not in my classroom.

Recognizing something was wrong, I tried to call my mother to tell her what was happening, but I couldn't connect, and didn't want to ask my roommate for help. Thinking of the many years I had called that number, and the mix up now, I just gave up, completely frustrated.

My next memory was when I woke up in a darkened room with the bars on the windows as already mentioned, knowing hardly anything. That part of me called *self* was shaken and there was no answer to what caused it. Everything I had ever done and experienced was what made me my *self*, those things that made me the very being that I was. I tried to summon my *self* like I used to, to no avail. My gynecologist had been coming to the psych ward to change my bandage because he said I had contracted an infection in the tissue. Then I vaguely remembered trying to rip my bandage off.

I thought I knew myself pretty well, but I had never had these problems before. My self seemed disconnected. I couldn't connect anything like I used to. I had no notion to pray and no conscious knowledge of God or my faith. But I did know a traumatic event had happened.

Days passed as I continued getting acclimated to the psychiatric ward. My psychiatrist soon suggested a weekend at my home to see how I would do, and I agreed. Upon my return, he discussed discharge, which I welcomed, but the thought that I might not be able to go back to work didn't settle well with me. He also told me after taking the prescribed medications along with seeing a psychiatrist for several years, that I might be able to discontinue the medications.

Well, I have never liked taking medication. As a child, I used to throw it behind the kitchen stove. Now, I'd just have to learn how to swallow it. My only glimpse of anything like this happening to anyone was my vague memory of the movie, "What Ever Happened to Baby Jane," produced by Warner Brothers. However, I found consolation that my *self* was only shaken, not completely shattered, by the fact that I knew my name when I woke up in that room. Things began to come back together. Knowing my name also let me know that the knowledge of God was still in my heart as it too came back later. The mind can play tricks on you, but I hid things in my heart. Furthermore, knowing my name proved to me that Hebrews 13:5 was true, "God will never leave thee nor forsake thee." My *self* may have been shaken, but not my faith. I was reminded of Paul's writing in the Bible, Romans 8:38-39, "For I am persuaded that neither death, nor life, nor angels, nor principalities, nor powers, nor things to come, nor height, nor depth, nor any other creature, shall be able to separate us from the love of God." My mission now turned to finding out what caused this unfortunate phenomenon in the first place.

Chapter 2

Pressing Forward: Drugs, Side Effects, And Related Divergences

CAUTIOUSLY PRESSING MY WAY AFTER DIS-charge, I knew I never wanted to lose that sense of *self* again. Moreover, the doctors didn't know what caused the loss, but my psychiatrist prescribed Valium, a drug I'd never heard of. Before this event, I didn't even know what a tranquilizer was.

Perhaps like any other average person who had always been healthy, the differences between regular over-the-counter drugs, prescribed meds, and psychotropic drugs (and their side effects) were not widely known. Whereas it took maybe thirty minutes for an Anacin/Bufferin combination to deliver its therapeutic effect, I learned it might take several weeks for some psychotropic drugs. With the traumatic event still fresh on my mind, I reconciled my thinking. I'd just have to take things one day at a time, learning to adjust as much as possible along the way, but at the same time feeling in the back of my mind that this just might be a rather far-reaching undertaking.

I had never liked taking medicine. As a child, my mom would get so tired trying to get me to take it that she'd give up and leave the kitchen. Then I'd quickly throw it behind the stove; in my adult life, she told me that she found it. The problem for me was swallowing it. I'd gag or choke, but now I'd just have to learn how to swallow the medications. My consolation was the scripture Luke 18:27, "The things which are impossible with men are possible with God." Another scripture that helped me was Philippians 4:13, "I can do all things through Christ which strengtheneth me." After taking Valium for two years, and basically regulating and cutting myself back from the high dose regimen, I settled on a plan that I thought was right for me. It allowed me to work in the day and also helped me sleep at night, but right away, the side effects especially affected my memory causing forgetfulness and embarrassment before I got used to handling them. In regular conversation, I'd sometimes lose my train of thought in the middle of a sentence, and when passing someone in the hall, I might not remember something shared with me by the time I got back to my room.

As time passed, and life continued to return to a more regular routine and normalcy, I began to better understand the extent and consequences of this unfortunate event. I had forgotten a lot of the French skills I'd learned starting in tenth grade and during college, so much that teaching it again was a more far off concept now. Nevertheless, I always had a deep love for studying and learning which was supported by the scriptures 2 Timothy 2:15, "Study to show thyself approved unto God, a workman that needeth not be ashamed, rightly dividing the word of truth," and also Ecclesiastes 3:1, "To everything there is a season, and a time to every purpose under the heaven." I am glad that I learned at the appropriate time, place, and season that was right for me, but now I found myself in a season of my life unable to read the French literature books that I saved in college to read in my leisure in my adult life. I decided not to cry over spilled milk, but rather my mind turned to gratitude for the visionary teaching at my dedicated historically black college (HBCU) undergraduate school where everyone was advised to have a major and a minor area of study to graduate. That advice served me well, even until now; have a plan B, because as fate would have it, my natural English reading skills were also somewhat impacted. My reading speed and comprehension slowed a bit, but not like my French. I still had enough English know-how requirements for something, and so I focused on the, "Yes, I can," and not on what I didn't have left. The, "ram in the bush," described in Genesis 22: 1-14 was at work for me.

Continuing to adjust, I discovered that not only was my memory greatly affected, but my energy level had declined. I was always tired and weak, yet could seldom take a nap. Then there were those times, feeling utter exhaustion like I was going to just drop, when I would be overtaken by a one or two minute nap. For those times, I thanked the Lord. First, that my natural sleep function was not completely damaged, and second, such rare moments made me very happy as though I'd just received a treasured gift. Third, I'd get a very refreshed feeling like I'd had adequate, restful sleep. To further cope with always trying to remember better, I'd write down the meds I'd take every day, and how I felt. In light of not knowing if or when I'd have a repeat episode of my *self* in shambles, for which the cause was still unknown, this habit gave me a running account of progress or at least a documented account of how the day before had gone.

I used to like to pray aloud in church service because I had always prayed at least once a day before going to sleep at night, and had done that since my parents taught me my first prayer, "Now I lay me down to sleep. I pray the Lord my soul to keep. If I should die before I wake, I pray the Lord my soul to take." I had to stop praying aloud in church for fear of forgetting in front of the whole congregation. Sometimes my childhood prayer would be the only one I could pray at night. This was another consequence of the unfortunate event. So I took on another church responsibility, which was calling the church office to give the church bus driver the names of those who called the church office during the week to request pick up for the eleven o'clock Sunday service. I also made another call reminding members of their prior commitment to read the Sunday lessons for the day. Like this, my participation in the very life of the church was still possible despite my memory problem. Plus, I got a good feeling talking to someone else from church.

There were numerous other side effects and drug-related divergences that lasted for varying periods: a day, a week, or years. I took Halcion for sleep every night for seven years at one point, even though after some time, it only allowed me to sleep about three hours a night. I wondered what would have happened without it. Restoril and Ambien (also sleep medications) were also a part of my treatment at different times. Thinking back, I'm reminded of a sermon preached by a very young preacher named Clinton. The name of the sermon was "Sometimes You Just Have to Press your Way," and it gave me the impetus I needed many times to help spur myself along like from a caffeine drink.

Other multiple side effects were:

- Dry mouth.
- Palpitations.
- Brain feeling like it was in a fog.
- Feeling like I had a head cold.
- Inability to wind down. Feeling like I could just explode, or like a rubber band being stretched to its limits.
- A feeling of trying to carry a tub of water up the stairs (especially sometimes the next day after taking Halcion).
- Feeling that I appeared rude with no manners, blurting into conversations. Trying to express my point of view before it left my mind (holding my thoughts until someone else finished speaking wasn't as easy as it used to be).
- Trying unsuccessfully to make plans in my head (a thought might leave before I could connect it to the other thoughts to store and retrieve later).
- Always needing to write down the directions, both going and coming back when driving to any new place that required making two or three turns.
- Suddenly forgetting where I was (momentarily) while driving. This was especially troubling when remembering a woman I knew in Detroit who was found in another city and didn't know where she was.
- Being accused of pretending to have memory loss.
- Falling into a recurring trance of some kind, or nightmares lasting thirty or forty-five minutes. Not always knowing where I was in the trance. Sometimes I couldn't come out of these very easily, especially when I was feeling really tired.

- Catching myself, but not often, just staring or gazing at the wall or into space.
- Always having to make a special effort to appear alert when engaging with people, my children, and then later, my grandchildren.

Life still had to be lived, each moment, facing whatever happened each day the best I could. Continuing to thank the Lord for the psychiatrists, the medications, and my faith for working together to keep my *self* unshaken and intact, I pressed on. The scripture Isaiah 40:29 was always helpful, "He giveth power to the faint, and to them that have no might, he increaseth strength." I read that often. It was calming during the times when I'd think or feel like I might slip out of control, and the times when I'd think or feel like I might slip out of control from reality little by little became less and less.

Then, a remarkable turn of events happened. I was hospitalized for a second C-section. I told the nurse, "I feel like I'm going to go through the same thing that happened four years ago because the wall just moved up to the foot of my bed." This scared me. I knew I was hallucinating. The nurse responded, "We might need to check your Demerol. I'll check with your doctor." The clue...suddenly, this was the clue...Demerol. I just knew it in my spirit. Never having heard this word before, I sensed this was the revelation from God I'd been waiting for over the past four years. Thus, before the nurse returned, I'd already decided to decline any more Demerol. They discontinued it, and instead started me on codeine by mouth which caused itching, hives, and an allergic reaction. Consequently, I asked for an Anacin/Bufferin combination for pain, which I think they eventually gave me, but I had to go through a whole other series of injections to counteract the allergic reaction. Still of paramount importance, I didn't go out of my head. Even more importantly, I now knew it was the Demerol (at least I thought it was) because the wall did not move back to the foot of my hospital bed anymore after it was discontinued. I credited my conscientious nurse for this. Perhaps she read something in my chart, but my quest was yielding the desired outcome.

With unremitting devotion, I continued the Valium, and as life would have it, my family soon relocated to Detroit from Gary, Indiana. My third C-section was performed the following year. I was very anxious at the thought of having complications again with a new doctor, at a new hospital, and in another city. My doctor in Michigan arranged for me to travel back to Indiana to be cared for by the same doctors that were involved with my prior complications. My doctors in Indiana did a spinal procedure, and I stayed awake; no Demerol and no loss of control of reality. As things progressed back in Detroit, it became apparent that despite the good news about the Demerol, the new relocation ushered in a new round of challenging responsibilities. I now had three children, and I had worked my way from a clerical I position to an executive secretary III. Trying to coordinate everything, I got a little slack, not taking time to refill the Valium I'd been taking for seventeen years. This led to me trying to ration my pills a little too long before a trip to my doctor's office. I didn't realize the consequences this could cause. I had the feeling that the FBI was after me. The feeling just crept up on me.

One day, the conference room at my job had been crowded with many people standing around talking and it frightened me. I told my husband that I wanted to talk to a lawyer, but he said let's see the doctor first. At the doctor's office, it looked like everyone except the doctor was wearing a mask, but I didn't mention that to anyone. I just didn't know what to make of it. Instead of refilling the Valium, Sinequan was prescribed four times a day, as well as rest from work (temporarily), which was the new treatment plan which I followed. In a couple of months or so, my doctor told me to discontinue Sinequan, and I complied.

Things seemed normal the first few days. There were no masks on people, but then once again, though slowly, unusual things started happening. I realized that I was spiraling down another out-of-control path with intermittent bizarre behavior and thoughts. My husband became concerned about my behavior and called the doctor who gave him the name of a psychiatrist to hospitalize me. I signed myself in and was admitted for two or three weeks.

In retrospect, I thought that because discontinuing the Demerol during my second C-section stopped my hallucinations of the moving wall, and then not going out of my head after avoiding Demerol altogether with a spinal procedure for my third and last C-section, proved that it was the Demerol that caused the unexpected phenomenon of my *self* in shambles that made this treatment path necessary in the first place.

Hence, this new concern, baffling to say the least, made me have a new batch of questions. It also made me have to take many more medications, and they had new side effects that required additional new medications, such as Stelazine, Cogentin, Temazepam, Meclizine, and whatever else. The new psychiatrist said that this most recent event was caused by a chemical imbalance, but the cause of the imbalance was unknown. Other new terms describing my illness were bipolar and major depression, but always depression. I was a librarian and I always wanted to know all that I could, so I purchased the *"Physician's Desk Reference"* (PDR). I wanted to better understand the new side effects and other related terminology. In the meantime, one new medication caused the most intolerable effect I'd experienced so far. I couldn't sit still for more than two or three minutes before having to get up and pace around. Fortunately, this was during hospitalization, and my roommate told me that she had the same reaction to Haldol. Luckily, the misery was short-lived because the psychiatrist was already at the hospital, and changed or discontinued the drug without delay. This one finding in itself made the purchase of the PDR well worth the investment. Now when prescribed a new drug, I check the PDR to learn about the side effects before purchasing the drug. I'm much savvier now, as well as more apprehensive about taking new medicines than I used to be.

Contemplating all that had to be considered over the years, every day my concern was making the best of what God had given me because I didn't have the right to take my feelings out on anyone else. As the old people used to say, "You get it in your head, and nobody can take it away." Well, the initiative for this book began as a quest to find out what tried to take mine away. If it wasn't Demerol or the abrupt stoppage of Sinequan, then what? I thought a repeat episode of losing control of reality was no longer a concern after not encountering the adverse effects of Demerol during my last two C-sections. My quest continued since the loss happened again after stopping Sinequan. Through all this, I've developed my own theory. Now, being introduced to information about a new possibility from an oral surgeon regarding my possible sensitivity to opioids like Demerol, and as a small, framed person, I may have had too much build up in my system. I've listened to others' opinions all these years. Let me sum up this chapter. The two drugs I've felt best about were Valium and Amitriptyline. Valium served me well for seventeen years all while raising my three children and working, and Amitriptyline (from my understanding) protects the brain and better stimulates new brain cell growth. I actually felt the brain cell stimulation, like I could study again. Moreover, the Levoxyl and Amitriptyline combination seemed to have real promise. With the first dose, I slept seven hours straight the first night and woke up refreshed like I used to feel when much younger. My mind was just as sharp. I had felt bad for so long that I didn't remember how it was to feel good again. The *magic pill*; I thought we'd finally found it, and I was prepared to take the Amitriptyline, and Perphenazine for a long time to come, but my psychiatrist said research showed that Amitriptyline could cause increases in blood pressure causing a stroke, and so it was discontinued. What I can say is that I haven't had that many headaches all these years on this treatment, just some dizziness at times.

Information on all the drugs mentioned in this chapter and others can be found in the PDR in the reference section of the public library or online at the reference desk. So far, for the most serious life-threatening side effects I've experienced, I was informed only after the fact; Opioids, Fentanyl, etc. are in the news now. My Amitriptyline interacted with Fentanyl during a transesophageal echocardiogram study I was undergoing due to a mini-stroke. I was told that I'd be in a twilight state, but with the IV Fentanyl, I stopped breathing one minute into the study, and they had to stop the test and give me Romazicon and Narcan to bring me back. After they told me all that, I declined to reschedule the test. I learned more about Fentanyl later from the TV news reporting on the death of the musician, Prince. I didn't know all this about the central nervous system suppressants and interactions with psychotropic meds making the compound more potent.

Before the traumatic event, I was healthy and had taken very little medicine at age twenty-six other than vitamins, but I was not spared from suicidal ideations sometimes. I learned that some of the medications themselves could cause it. This wasn't even a fleeting thought ever before, but, "Do it! Do it! Do it!" was a strong urge in my mind one day. However, my concern was always who would find me, and how could that affect them? The Lord wasn't ready for me yet, and I now think of all that I would have missed.

In conclusion, a second life-threatening episode occurred again with Amitriptyline and Perphenazine interacting with the opioid medicine Dilaudid after a hysterectomy. I had a weak pulse and then experienced respiratory and cardiac arrest. I was given Narcan twice at the suggestion of my daughter, an RN, who was with me. The array of drugs over all this time helped me hold together some semblance of my core *self*, along with my faith and the scripture which I credit as the silver lining of it all, motivating me to listen to the voice within, "Yes, I can," and to press on. Eventually, the fear of slipping out of control didn't come to my mind as much.

I can say unequivocally that God's grace in my life has kept me. In 2 Corinthians 12:9 it says, "For my strength is made perfect in weakness." The doctors told me that they didn't know what caused my *self* to be in shambles, but Jeremiah 32:17 says, "Ah Lord God! Behold, thou hast made the heaven and the earth by thy great power and stretched out arm, and there is nothing too hard for thee." I believe in doctors' healing, God's ordinary healing, as well as His supernatural healing power.

Chapter 3

We Are Products Of Our Past

A REVIEW OF THE MANY DRUGS I'VE TAKEN, and their side effects for many years, has not led me to a definitive determination that could have contributed to or foreshadowed my unexpected and unexplained traumatic event as expounded in Chapter 1. That loss of control of reality, or my other way of putting it, my *self* in shambles spurs me on in this trek to find a clue that could have foreshadowed it.

Moving forward, I know very little about psychiatry, but I took an introduction to psychology class in college, and I associate the name Freud somewhere in that discipline. I also know from life that something that happens in one's past can affect future behavior. A therapist delving into a person's past might be able to shed more light on an area. Therefore, my mission looking back in my past from birth through adolescence, and through college for a clue to the cause continues.

Immediate Family

From the outset, I don't think I had a complicated or adverse family life. All of my experiences growing up with my parents and siblings made me *myself*, the very being that I was. Thereby in my thinking, the best place to start looking for a cause is life with my parents and siblings that helped form the *me*, and my way of thinking and developing from the beginning. My mom and dad were hard-working, loving parents who loved the Lord, their children, their extended family, and people in general. My dad and mom dated some off and on. It was hard to see each other in those days before many automobiles and during the cold winters. They were married on January 16, 1937, both descendants of slaves (see addendum). My oldest sister was born in November of 1938, and my second sister in October of 1939. My dad was a soft-spoken, gentleman of small stature, but strong enough to lift heavy bags of fertilizer and to connect heavy farm equipment. The church was always an integral part of our lives. I heard my dad pray almost every Sunday at church, giving thanks to God first, then requesting, "Lord, bless everyone with the needs they stand in need of." This is a request that I still make in many of my prayers, especially for members of my immediate family.

Back then, we went to Sunday school and studied from Sunday school books every Sunday. We stayed for the eleven o'clock worship service every second Sunday. All my siblings and I eventually became baptized members of my father's church where we learned a lot. I still recall a Sunday school superintendent from way back who said almost every Sunday, "There're enough ways in the world for everybody to have one." So, I learned early on that adjusting to someone else's ways would require effort on my part too. That wise statement allowed me to tell my then toddler grandson, the same thing when he was around three years old, and expressed to me one day, seemingly out of the blue, and maybe after some deep thought, "Granny, the Lord made me the way that I am." I responded, "Yes, He did, and He said that what He made was very good" (Gen. 1:31, KJV). I added, "He made you like He wanted you."

Another thing I learned from church while very young was, "There is so much good in the worst of us, and so much bad in the best of us, that it behooves us all not to talk about the rest of us", by Robert Louis Stevenson. As was the case, even though my parents belonged to different churches before marriage, they continued to support each other's church afterward; my father's church on the second Sunday, and my mom's church on the third Sunday, until both churches started having worship services twice a month. This decision had great benefits for their four children. We were doubly blessed having more people to love us and look out for us from two anointed village congregations. As stated in the African culture, it takes a village to raise a child.

My father was a deacon and my mother a deaconess at my dad's church. He donated some of his land to build the church. He also kept some of the church's offerings back then before ATMs and bank arrangements. It wasn't as easy to go to the bank and other places back then, living out in the boondocks, before automobiles. My dad kept the church's money on his dresser. I remember stacks of quarters, nickels, dimes, and pennies, but the children knew not to bother any of it, not even a penny. My dad probably knew exactly how many pennies there were. One penny back then could buy some candy, a kit which was small, pink, sweet and hard kinda like a "now a later", but that Sunday school hymn, "Yield Not to Temptation" kept you honest. My parents didn't talk that much about a good feeling they got from the church, but they intentionally showed the presence of God in our home, among themselves, and with their four children. All of us were loved equally for one's self, making each of us feel that valuable self-worth. There were no demeaning or sarcastic statements, put-downs, or little lies out of frustration like, "I'll kill you," or, "You're getting on my last nerve."

There were celebrations on holidays, especially Thanksgiving, Christmas, and Easter, but not Halloween. Of course, we believed in Santa Claus. On Christmas Eve, we were sure to have saved a good, sturdy, cardboard box from the packhouse to place in the living room with our Christmas lists inside. You might get at least one thing on your list, but it was mostly socks, notebooks, paper, pencils, nuts, candy, apples, oranges, and things you needed. I can remember being so highly excited watching the skies one Christmas Eve that I was certain I saw Santa in his sleigh, and reindeer flying around the chimney over the top of our two-story house. Where could you find an aberration in this upbringing so far; wholesome, positive building of the *self*? No clue in my quest.

Then one Sunday evening, things changed. My mom's good friend, a cousin on my daddy's side, came to our house to visit. I was bubbling over because she used to always tell me in the churchyard how pretty I looked in my pretty dress with the sash and matching bows on my three braids. She didn't have any children and said that she wanted me to be her little girl. Well, to my surprise and broken heart, she didn't pay me any attention at my house. I had to stay in another room while they visited in the living room. I realize now that I was too young to be able to reason back then, that there were no telephones and no way for adults to have a confidential con-versation about perhaps someone's sickness, someone's bad behavior, or whatever the issue that was inappropriate for a young child like me to hear. I couldn't reason about any of that as a child.

As I stated, this cousin was so friendly to me in front of my dad and mom in the churchyard. This was my first time experiencing such an about-face toward me from anyone I thought was so special, not from an aunt or anyone. I didn't understand it. I just kept going to the swinging double doors between the living and dining room peeping in the living room, and my mom would say, "I see you," which I didn't realize. Finally, she said, "Come on in, Alice," which just thrilled me to bring my little rocking chair in and be near the person who treated me so special. They began to include me in the conversation with all smiles, making me feel really good.

Then after some time, the guests prepared to leave, and to my disappointment after they left, my mom changed from smiling to chastising me, and she gave me a whipping. It was the first whipping I can remember getting. "Children are to be seen and not heard," was the culture back then and I had to learn and understand that lesson suddenly that night, the hard way. To speculate in retrospect about what I've learned as an adult now with children of my own, about the part called *self*, and how it develops after you're born, and as a toddler, I imagine I was possibly just beginning to be aware of my physical self as *me*, separate from others, and also becoming aware of the psychological attributes of myself to have expectations of getting the same treatment from my mom's friend every time. I expected her to tell me that I was looking pretty and that I was special. Instead, I had to understand the first shock of my physical being, a whipping. I now knew *me*, and that I was separate from others.

Even though I was little, these happenings impacted me so profoundly as to make me decide then and there if I ever had children, they would not be relegated to another room, but my guests would have to pay attention to my children as well as to me, and I made it so.

Despite this happening to me as a toddler, I knew my parents loved me, and showed this love in countless ways. I don't know whether this incident did or did not alter my psyche. I just know at the time, my two or three-year-old *self* didn't feel good. That evening in particular wasn't a positive builder of my toddler *self*. I had to learn and get used to the different ways and personalities of grown-ups. I had never felt this way with my siblings. Moving right along, time passed as

I grew and learned more about the complexities of other adult human beings.

The Thing at the Foot of the Bed

Turning now to another experience, *the thing at the foot of the bed* began to terrorize me every night in the two-story house which was our home. The house was built by my grandfather for his family around 1790, toward the end of slavery. It was a picturesque site, just perfect to raise a family. My grandfather cut the trees with his bare hands.

There was a medium-sized kitchen, a living room, and a dining room on the first floor divided by stairs, and a long hall running beside it, with my parent's bedroom and a little room on the other side. At some time, my only brother who was two years younger than me was born and they called me the knee baby. My brother was always in my mom's lap, and I hovered around her and my dad's knees. I slept in the little room in a full-sized bed between my two sisters. I felt pretty safe from falling off the bed, snuggled down between my sisters, but this one thing still terrorized me every night. It would come and make loud, monstrous noises in the hall; I imagined perhaps something from out of the nearby woods. At times, there was talk of a bear sighting, and the noise was indeed loud enough to be a bear, and a pig snorting, then squealing. At other times, just shrill high and low sounds, then a return to monstrous. It was scary.

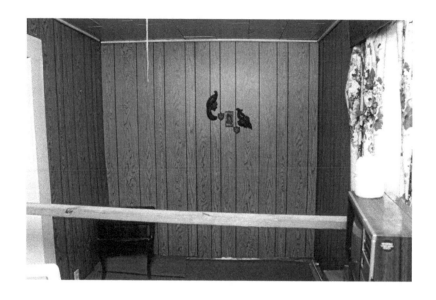

Then one night, I'd just had it. I was tired, rest-broken, and fed up. The creature didn't seem to faze my sisters, but I was at my turning point and determined to do something. At last, I summoned all the courage I could muster, and slowly, quietly pushed open the little room door so it wouldn't squeak. I was cringing and afraid something was going to jump out at me. It was so dark. I can't remember if we had electricity by then or still used lanterns or lamps, but so far, so good, nothing jumped out. So I tiptoed around the bottom of the stairs out in the hall and paused. The noise seemed to get louder and louder as I crept up the hall towards my parent's room. Inching still closer, the noise got even louder, but then softer again. Then to my surprise and consolation, it became clear; it was my father snoring, and had been all those nights before. Mission accomplished! I turned and ran back to bed between my sisters, feeling greatly relieved and proud of myself.

Sometime later, a door was cut and hung in the wall between my parents' and the girls' room. No longer did I have to go up the long hallway to reach my parents' room, but I had learned a good lesson. Even being little and having no power, if you face your fears, you just might end up better off. It was a great confidence builder for my all-important *self*. No clue, foreshadowing, of my *self* in shambles yet.

Continuing forward and diverting again a bit, my father had to drop out of school in the eighth grade and began running the farm after my grandfather's stroke. Just like my grandfather, my father cared for the home site with fruit trees, walnut trees, grapevines, etc., that surrounded our home. My dad planted a big garden every year, just like my grandfather, with tomatoes, green beans, butter beans, okra, and cabbage which helped supply most of the family's needs. The garden of Adam and Eve couldn't have been much more beautiful. We wanted for nothing.

The Work Ethic

From this backdrop, my parents taught us how to work from an early age; because there was work on the farm for everyone. As soon as you could walk and bend down without falling, some chickens would be glad to get a grain or two of corn from a little person brave enough to throw it, and if you could pick up a toy, you were able to pick up a leaf of green tobacco off the dirt floor under the barn shelter on tobacco day. I helped do all this along with my other siblings. These simple jobs developed a can-do, yes I can attitude.

This was my world. We had pigs, a mule named Kate, and a cow named Sook. I watched my dad and mom gather slop (old left-over food) combined with dishwater to feed the pigs every day. My dad also fed the mule and milked the cow that he also put out to pasture every day on her stake. Sometimes, I'd go with him to feed the animals, and was simply fascinated watching them eating. What in this world of mine could have foreshadowed my unfortunate episode years later, I can only guess.

Danger

I thought I didn't have a complicated family life, but rather an ordinary childhood. Then one day, I heard my sisters screaming at the top of their lungs, and I rushed to the back door to see what was happening. The cow had broken loose from her stake and was chasing them. All I could do was watch, frozen, spell-bound, and cowering behind my mom. The cow kept gaining speed on them as they ran as fast as they could. It looked like the cow's nose was just a few inches from a loose string of yarn on the back of my sister's red, wool sweater. It seemed she was just about to be slaughtered when my mom flung the door open and they fell inside just in time as the cow ran past. My dad had told us not to taunt and throw rocks at the cow on her stake. I just don't know what caused the cow to break loose that day, but they were in grave danger. This frightened me to no end, but I don't think this was any foreshadowing of my traumatic episode.

Starting School and Branching Out

I kept growing and my baby brother grew fast also. I was very glad to have a playmate close to my size, like my two sisters who were closer to each other in size. Another stage of my life was about to begin. I'd wanted to be like my sisters for a long time and walk to the two-room unpainted school with them, but first I had to learn my ABC's, and I did.

My dad would work with me on this project after coming in all tired from a day in the fields and about. I would look at the ABC board and say each letter as he pointed to them. I was already self-motivated, but he also had a switch in one hand that I cannot remember him using. Just the sight of it created a constant incentive that helped me remember. Now as I look back, I wonder if these early learning sessions with him may very well have helped me develop the desire to always do well.

When the big day finally came, I was simply thrilled. I was almost five years old. We walked down the dirt roads past the sparse population of farmhouses and fields, past the community church to the old schoolhouse. Miss Ashford was the first, second, and third-grade teacher, and all those grades were in one room. I was very excited to see all the different crayons and liked coloring the pictures. Everything about being at school excited me. My class was small, and my first cousin Doris and about three other girls from the community were in my class.

One weekend, Miss Ashford invited me to her home and I went to her church one of those nights where they washed your feet. This was the first time I had ever had my feet washed at church, though I had heard of this practice. Though I enjoyed the visit, I did not spend another weekend with her.

My brother soon started going to the two-room school also. Recess was a lot of fun when everyone in the school went outside together. One day, I wanted to play jump board with a girl heavier than me because her extra weight would propel me higher in the air and I liked that. The jump board was a long board laid across a cinder block or some other sturdy object. As my friend and I took turns jumping each other into the air, it was great fun, but then amid all the fun, my heavier partner on the other end propelled me high up; seemingly, high enough to touch the tree limbs. Unfortunately, my foot slipped and I missed the board coming down and fell to the ground so hard it momentarily knocked my breath out. I'm sure this probably also fractured my wrist because it was so sore that I could barely pick up the plants to help my dad set them out in the field that evening, but I couldn't tell my parents I had hurt myself at school on the jump board. I don't know if my brother told them, but he admonished me, "Mama told you not to be out there playing on that jump board." I don't remember getting on it again. My wrist was sore for many days, maybe even two or three weeks.

Though there were scary times and some danger, to repeat, I feel I had a normal family life, not an adverse upbringing. My siblings and I worked hard and were raised with a high regard for education, and a high reverence for God. We had a table in the dining room where all of us studied. There was also a fireplace in the dining room.

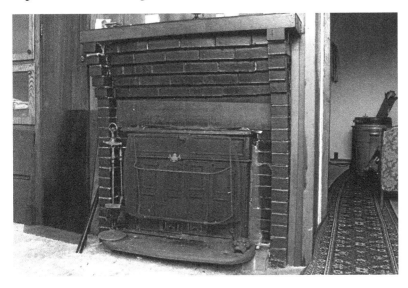

My dad put even more emphasis on studying since he had dropped out of school in the eighth grade, As a child, my mom attended school at Bakers Branch. She graduated from Douglass High School in eleventh-grade, valedictorian in 1934, and wanted to go to college, but her oldest sister who graduated the same year had a disfiguring burn on her face and was chosen to go instead. My grandfather and grandmother had decided beforehand that they wanted their first child to go to college so she could be independent, and would not have to depend on a husband because of her disfigurement.

My grandmother died in childbirth leaving eight children. My mother kept her siblings and took on the household duties of a mother at age sixteen. Back then, they advanced students to grades, and my mother had been advanced to the same grade as her oldest sister.

Moving along, as I recall, my father helped me with homework as needed until the fifth grade and my mom until the eighth grade. I cannot remember help with homework after eighth grade, but my mother liked to recite poems to us. "If" by Rudyard Kipling, and "Be the Best of Whatever You Are", by Douglas Malloch, were my favorites. I also loved to hear my Aunt Al, a senior class English teacher, recite "Mother to Son." "Well son, I'll tell you: Life for me ain't been no crystal stair... but I'se still climbing on..." by Langston Hughes. These recitations helped me develop a love of language and literature. My mom also told us she used to walk fourteen miles to school, and fourteen miles back home every day. They memorized long poems and had oratorical contests in school as part of English class. She was very good at oratory speaking and was asked to speak at varied church and other community functions sometimes. She told me how they used to bake an oven full of sweet potatoes back then, and could take one to the field to have at work, and other places to eat hot or cold. To me, sweet potatoes played the role then a lot like fast-food restaurants do today.

If—

If you can keep your head when all about you
Are losing theirs and blaming it on you;
If you can trust yourself when all men doubt you,
But make allowance for their doubting too;
If you can wait and not be tired by waiting,
Or, being lied about, don't deal in lies,
Or, being hated, don't give way to hating,
And yet don't look too good, nor talk too wise;

If you can dream—and not make dreams your master;
If you can think—and not make thoughts your aim;
If you can meet with triumph and disaster
And treat those two impostors just the same;

If you can bear to hear the truth you've spoken
Twisted by knaves to make a trap for fools,
Or watch the things you gave your life to be broken,
And stoop and build'em up with worn-out tools;

If you can make one heap of all your winnings
And risk it on one turn of pitch-and-toss,
And lose, and start again at your beginnings
And never breathe a word about your loss;

If you can force your heart and nerve and sinew
To serve your turn long after they are gone,

And so hold on when there is nothing in you
Except the Will which says to them: "Hold on";

If you can talk with crowds and keep your virtue,
Or walk with kings—nor lose the common touch;
If neither foes nor loving friends can hurt you;
If all men count with you, but none too much;

If you can fill the unforgiving minute
With sixty seconds' worth of distance run—
Yours is the Earth and everything that's in it,
And—which is more—you'll be a Man, my son!

- Rudyard Kipling

Be the Best of Whatever You Are

If you can't be a pine on the top of a hill
Be a scrub in the valley—but be
The best little scrub on the side of the hill,
Be a bush if you can't be a tree.
If you can't be a highway just be a trail
If you can't be the sun be a star;
It isn't by size that you win or fail—
Be the best of whatever you are.

- Douglas Malloch

Mother to Son

Well, son, I'll tell you:
Life for me ain't been no crystal stair.
It's had tacks in it,
And splinters,
And boards torn up,

And places with no carpet on the floor—
Bare.
But all the time
I'se been a-climbin on,
And reachin' landin's,
And turnin' corners,
And sometimes goin' in the dark
Where there ain't been no light.
So boy, don't you turn back.
Don't you set down on the steps
'Cause you finds it's kinder hard.
Don't you fall now—
For I'se still goin', honey,
I'se still climbin',
And life for me ain't been no crystal stair.

- Langston Hughes

Chapter 4

Up And Becoming

S PREADING MY WINGS DESCRIBES THE NEXT stage of my life: in fourth grade trying to master the multiplication tables, more work on the farm, managing free-time, and varied other changes, but still much of the same. So far, there's still mostly nothing that I think could have foreshadowed my unexpected and unexplained traumatic event, and so my quest continued. On the contrary, in pointing to trauma ahead, most of my experiences continue to affirm a solid building of my so important *self*. The essentials that made my very own being, *me*, distinguishable from others; my parents and siblings always still supplying that unwavering basic support with expanding input now from more new friends and dedicated teachers.

My last year attending the two-room country school went by fast, and being bigger now, more was expected of me. In addition to working on our family farm, my father, as I recall, one year rented acreage from another farmer to grow more tobacco to help provide for our growing family's needs and future aspirations for college. This was a very important goal for my siblings and me.

Tobacco

Tobacco was the highest money-making crop. It required the most work, the biggest workforce, and equipment. My dad may or may not have been approved for a loan for seed money for planting and harvesting the tobacco, and so we grew produce, especially peppers and cucumbers to sell at the farmer's produce market. This helped provide for the general day-to-day family expenses until tobacco could be sold.

On tobacco day, the work might start at 4 a.m. and last until 9 p.m. Croppers, usually male teens and men, would take the bottom-most yellow/green leaves off each stalk in the field once a week. They'd put the leaves under their arms until they got an arm full, and then put them in the field truck. It was then pulled to the barn by the mule at first, then by a tractor years later. At the barn, two or three leaves were picked up off the barn table and passed to a person who tied them on a tobacco stick with tobacco string. Usually, girls and women, younger children, and older women stood and did this. The stick of yellow/green tobacco leaves was then hung on tiers in the barn and heated by a furnace and pipes called flues. The leaves turned shades of yellow to reddish-orange when they dried out.

As you can see, there was much handling of the tobacco on tobacco day. We'd take the sticks out of the barn and put them in another building called the packhouse until they were graded and taken to market to sell at the warehouse, usually out of town. Auctioneers would come by and look at it and buy it by the pound. It would have to be loaded on the farmer's truck and covered with canvasses, then tied with ropes for the trip to the warehouse where it was unloaded. Sometimes my dad had to stay a day or two at the market.

We four children didn't get paid an allowance for our work when we were young, but every Saturday night, my dad took us to town for about an hour. He gave us money to purchase something small. I was usually very happy to buy a scoop of peanuts and a yard of ribbon for my hair for church on Sunday. I aspired to work at the five and dime store, but there were only white cashiers.

There was something to do every day. We alternated between picking peppers and cucumbers, etc., and harvesting tobacco on different days throughout the growing and harvesting seasons which overlapped. We'd get up early in the morning to pick the peppers and cucumbers. As small as I was, I'd choose a bucket that wouldn't be too heavy for me when full, and then empty it into a bushel basket.

Although I never complained, the grandfather clock on the mantel in the living room usually kept me awake striking ten times, then twelve times at midnight, then one o'clock, and so on until 4 a.m. Often, it seemed like I'd just gotten to sleep when it was time to get up, and yet, I never thought to ask anyone else if the ticking and striking bothered them until I was grown. Through college and even now, a ticking clock in the room bothers me and keeps me awake.

Moving on, sometimes my dad would have a truckload of produce selling for fifty cents to five dollars or more each; though at the grocery store, one pod of green pepper might cost fifty cents (the same as we'd get paid sometimes for a whole bushel). You could see my dad's disappointment when a truckload sold for only fifty cents a bushel. He'd frown and shake his head and say, "they just took it." He didn't usually try to save the load overnight, or take it back the next day, or throw it out as some farmers did. He just took the lower price and we'd go on to something else. Things usually worked out so we'd have enough. My dad told us how some farmers would give a ham and get a good price from the auctioneer.

The work was hard but we also had fun. One game we played was we'd race to see who could pick a basket of peppers the fastest. Intertwined with fun though, there was also fear. One time in the cucumber patch, my sister Rosa asked, "Why do you keep throwing rocks at my pail?" All of a sudden, she jumped across two or three rows in one leap before stopping. As it turned out, it was not me, but a snake hitting her pail the whole time.

In addition to tobacco, peppers, and cucumbers to sell, we grew sweet potatoes, white potatoes, corn, etc. Inside the house after work in the fields, we washed jars: pints, quarts, half gallon sizes, and some smaller. We used them to can food for the winter. Some of the jars were hard to wash, and sometimes your hand might get stuck, but by wiggling it around you'd always get it out. My dad would buy bushels of peaches and apples that had to be peeled and canned. Also, we'd go into the woods with our buckets to pick blueberries. It was very tempting to eat too many while picking. The smell of a pan of freshly baked biscuits and a jar of blueberries or peaches from the pantry made a delicious snack many nights.

41

We were not privy to a lot of fast-food restaurants, but when a Dairy Queen was built, we enjoyed going there after working in the fields or whenever. Life was good.

First Job

Somewhere around eight years old, or between fourth and fifth grade, my parents allowed me to start working for other relatives in tobacco for pay. At summer's end of that first year, I had a ten-dollar bill that I'd been able to save, but the whole situation was bittersweet. One night riding in the car to visit relatives and holding the ten-dollar bill in my hand, I threw a wad of chewing gum out the car window, and inadvertently, the money with it. The road was pitch black except when passing another car. So I knew not to ask my dad to stop to find my money. Besides, I was too embarrassed to tell what I'd done. Besides, the ditch beside the road could have a snake in it, poison ivy, or some other prickly briers. This loss hurt badly, and it was something I'd done to myself. I just had to gather my wits and suck it up. There was no one but myself to blame. The learning curve was very steep. Up to this point, experiences had been mostly fun and hard work, but no clue leading to a foreshadowing of my reason for this quest.

Death of Clarice

As fate would have it, a tragic thing happened to my first cousin, Clarice. She and I were about the same age and enjoyed playing together. One day, as she was crossing the highway in front of her house coming home from school, a car hit and killed her. This was very sad. There isn't anything else much I can remember about this period of my life: not going to the funeral or anything, but my parents sent me to live with her mother, my aunt, for a time. I guess to try and help her with her grief.

She taught fifth grade and I was put in her class. I don't remember if she whipped me in her class or just used me as an example to help discipline her students by telling them if she'd whip her own niece, she'd whip them. It was something along those lines about whipping. The only other thing that comes to my mind now about my stay with her is that I fell off the bicycle and skinned my knee at her house. At some point shortly thereafter, my parents came and got me to come back home and live. In retrospect, I must have missed my family, but I can't remember.

Soon I started going to the city schools, still in fifth grade where Miss Clark was my teacher. The first day in her class without any warning, I felt a sting on my leg from her yardstick and didn't know why. The reason I learned later was for looking in the dictionary to write the meaning of a word. I'd never been asked to define words at the two-room country school, and don't recall such an assignment from my short stay in my aunt's fifth-grade class, but for some reason, I had my own dictionary under my desk the first day in Miss Clark's fifth-grade class at the city school. I had never been hit in a classroom by a teacher before that I can remember, and no one except my parents had hit me anyway. That's all I can remember about the fifth grade: my cousin's tragic death, something about a whipping in my aunt's class, and the surprise swat on the leg at the city school from Miss Clark's yardstick.

As already mentioned, I don't think I had a complicated family life or adverse childhood. In revisiting my past so far, the first whipping I ever got at two or three years old to teach the lesson that children are to be seen and not heard, coupled with the two references around whipping in my aunt's class, and Miss Clark's fifth grade class at the city school the first day, made me aware that there was something about whipping that didn't sit well with me. These experiences could very well have affected my psyche in the short term, but there were not many times, and so the positive experiences from my family overwhelmingly outweighed anything else.

I was happy growing up, and with my own children, whipping wasn't often an option I chose, and when I did, it was usually two swats in the hand with a thin switch. My son told me after being a grown man, "Mom what you did didn't hurt." I told him, "I wasn't trying to hurt you, just get your attention, and two swats usually got it."

The next big thing in my life in fifth grade was starting piano lessons. Upon reflection, this was a very good thing, coming at a good time, after all that happened (the recent death of my cousin/playmate, and whipping in school), especially considering all the good things that listening to music can do. Sally Francis, my cousin, was my first teacher. She played for Sunday school but would be leaving for college, and so they began grooming me to take her place. I was very happy about this because I had been going to church and Sunday school at this Baptist church ever since birth.

The *Gospel Pearl* was my first music book from which I learned to read notes. The first songs I learned to play were hymns, "Be Not Dismayed Whate'er Betide, God Will Take Care of You," "What a Friend We Have in Jesus," and, "Pass Me Not O Gentle Savior." They're still among my favorites. After some time, I was asked to learn some spiritual songs for the church choir and I got paid when I played for them, but not for Sunday school. I also began playing for weddings and got paid. I loved doing all of this; however, I was always a little nervous playing for the choir and weddings.

Continuing to evaluate the past, my brother and I started spending more time together because we were now at the same school. Rosa, the sister next to me in age, was still in high school, and my older sister was in college. Even though I was older than my brother, he was bigger, braver, and maybe in some ways wiser, I now confess. He always felt he had to look out for his sisters. My father had gotten special permission from the city school superintendent for my brother and me to attend there, which was out of our school district. He did this so that we could have more time to help work on the farm after school, and not spend all that time riding the county school bus home.

There was no city school bus running past our house. It only ran to a certain point to the end of the city limits, and we had to get off and walk the rest of the way home which was a good distance. One day we had to walk that long distance and passed a big house on the hill where we encountered a big bulldog. White people lived there. The big dog saw us coming from way up the road and started barking at us. I was scared to pass him and the closer and closer we got to the house, the dog seemed to get more and more agitated, barking even more viciously and seemingly upset. The dog started running toward the road where we were walking faster and faster.

I was stymied in my tracks, very afraid for my brother and me, and not sure what was going to happen. Then suddenly, my brother reached down and picked up a little stick or twig (the only thing I saw on the road's shoulder), and started charging toward the fierce dog. Then to our great relief and good fortune, the dog stopped barking and running toward us, turned, and started running back up the hill to his house, and we walked on past. We didn't have to walk along there again. This certainly was a threat, but I don't think it rose to the object of this quest either. We were not hurt.

Hurricane Hazel

It seemed many days passed and nothing out of the ordinary happened, just farm work, school, church, piano lessons, piano practice, and so on. I was now in eighth grade and attending middle school, when one day coming home from school there was disturbing talk of a hurricane bringing destruction and possible loss of life. This sounded very different from a regular thunderstorm when we'd rush in from the fields or barns for shelter. Overwhelmingly, the hurricane just swooped down on our region that day. I had never experienced anything like it.

The wind whirled in all its fury, swaying the school bus from side to side. What was happening with my sisters and brother? I worried. They were also probably trying to make it home. I remember getting off the school bus faced with the strongest wind I'd ever encountered; constantly struggling to keep from being blown to the ground along the lane leading from the county road and our mailbox to my house.

I finally arrived at the edge of our front yard. Then still tugging, and tightly clutching my coat to keep it on, I made it to the back door, but could hardly pull the screen door open. It seemed unusually suctioned closed. Continuing to reposition myself, pushing and pulling with all my strength (the wind still just powerfully furious), the door snapped open, almost making me fall to the floor of the enclosed back porch. Highly relieved, at least safe from physical harm, I couldn't help but wonder about everyone else.

After some time I gathered my wits and looked out the dining room window and saw my sister, Rosa, rolling over and over, being blown by the excessively strong wind toward the ditch that ran partially around the farm. Thinking about the black snake seen at times around the ditch made me feel even more afraid for her.

Much later, I asked Rosa, "How did you feel?" She said that she was scared but just couldn't stop rolling. I can't remember what stopped her, but she said Dad came and got her. I can't remember where my brother and older sister were, but maybe she was away at college. The usual instruction for bad thunderstorms was to sit or lie down someplace and be quiet, and that's what I did, but I was still afraid because it felt like the top floor itself was creaking and swaying and might just give way.

This was a Category 4 hurricane with winds reaching 200 miles per hour. Years later, I learned it was the deadliest, costliest, hurricane in the 1954 hurricane season. In Haiti, 469 people were killed, there were ninety-five fatalities in the U.S., and about a thousand people were hurt. It certainly interrupted the routine for a while, causing $382 million in damages. On our farm, trees and crops still left in the field were blown over. The talk was that it was the worst storm ever seen in those parts. While I don't see this as a clue contributing to my unexpected phenomenon, it sure was a complicated, scary adventure.

High School

Moving on, I entered high school, and my passion for learning increased in ninth grade with more opportunities at school, and with some new experiences in home life. This heightened passion for learning had been greatly encouraged in eighth grade and carried over from the sincere and capable guidance and teaching of two dynamic black teachers, Miss Highsmith and Miss Pearsall. Though not quite certain, I think it was from them that I first heard what could have been our motto, "The mind is the master of the man. They can who think they can." Of course, my parents had instilled that in their children all along.

Since segregation was the law of the land, all my teachers thus far had been black, and as I look back, they believed we could learn and seemingly had no hang-ups about wanting to make a positive difference in all of us. I was never made to feel that I didn't belong or denied participation in class which I later experienced in graduate school, and I include in another chapter.

More mature but very petite, and still highly motivated, I experienced more firming up of future goals. I joined the band and learned to play the clarinet. I continued piano lessons, but with a new piano teacher, Miss Washington, who also directed the choir which I joined later as well.

It wasn't just the new classes in ninth grade that were a change. I had my first kiss in ninth grade with my first boyfriend, Robert Earl. My parents didn't allow me to go out on dates, and neither could my two older sisters. My boyfriend would come to my home and visit in the living room where we'd talk and watch TV. It was a small town and my boyfriend who lived in the city would sometimes get a ride to my house in the country from someone who knew my older sisters.

There were dances and parties at school for Valentine's Day, Christmas, homecoming, and the Explorer's Club. I can remember two artists, Sam Cooke and Fats Domino, whose records were played at the dances. I enjoyed dancing, and my dad usually took me and picked me up afterward. I loved all kinds of music and at home, watched *The Liberace Show* (a famous pianist), and *The Lawrence Welk Show* with my family. Later, *The Ed Sullivan Show* entertained us. I also enjoyed the *Amos 'n' Andy Show* and *The Little Rascals*. These are the only two Black shows I remember when we got a TV. Later, there was *I Love Lucy, not a Black show but very funny and enjoyable.*

Refocusing on the daytime scheduled activities in the tenth and eleventh grades, I added French and continued to mostly make the honor roll while still enjoying traveling with the band. It was especially exciting playing the second part on the piano with my piano teacher (where four hands were required), and while the choir sang, "The Battle Hymn of the Republic." The choir sang in many concerts at other schools and churches, and one time traveled out of state. It was my first time leaving the state for anything. In particular, I went to St. Petersburg, Florida with "The Mixed Group", about five choir members (a soprano, tenor, alto, bass ...) from the choir and saw a lot of things that dazzled my eyes. This was my first time riding on a glass-bottom boat, and I was nervous about it in the beginning because I couldn't swim. It was also my first time hearing the terminology "schools of fish." All of this was very important in the building of my *self*, a core part of my being. Surely, as I look back now, the travel did not contribute to my *self* in shambles as reported in Chapter 1. Instead, it built self-confidence.

My older sister went to college to become a nurse, and the sister next to me and I now shared the little room with the same full-sized bed as we three girls used to share. Rosa and I now had a lot more time to get closer doing farm work, etc. When we were younger, she was always the one who had compassion on me in the middle of the night and went with me to the outside toilet in the dark before we got electricity and an inside bathroom. I'm still so endeared to her for helping me way back then. Later, we would have a light fixture erected, and I would learn as a young adult that I had a milk allergy, lactose intolerance way back then too. Rosa and I had some of the same teachers, and I'll never forget the time she invited me to a meal in her home economics class, where I thoroughly enjoyed the food and everything I learned about home economics. They planned their menu, had a budget, bought the food and prepared it, and were taught table manners and table setting (real fine dining).

Rosa was a member of the New Homemakers of America (NHA) Club. It was for those who took home economics, and she was selected to represent the NHA and ride on its float. I was very happy for her. She looked really pretty on the float, and I wanted to someday be like her and ride on a float, just as I yearned to be like my sisters when starting first grade. The two of us still loved going downtown shopping on Saturday night, just walking around the town square, and sometimes running into friends from school, very much like malls today.

In the meantime, things changed a little in the family at some point. As fate would have it, my first cousin, James, came to live with us because his mother, my dad's sister, passed away leaving several minor children. James' father was an alcoholic so their children were taken in by the family, and other loving or capable adults. James didn't like to study and would sit at the dining room table and sleep while the rest of us studied. He couldn't read well, and there was talk of him going to barber college instead of a four-year college.

I remember how James helped on the farm and drove me to different places. One night I was with him and he drove to Club 117 in Goldsboro. Fats Domino was supposed to be there, but there was talk of a shooting outside, and I can't recall if we saw Fats Domino, and neither can I remember going there again. Another night, James took me someplace and there was a bridge we always crossed on the way home, but this time when approaching the bridge, to my surprise, James started accelerating. He pressed the accelerator over 100 mph going across the bridge. I was afraid and angry, but I knew my parents didn't know he would do that. Although thoroughly perplexed, I knew if I told on him, it would probably affect my going places because it would put more responsibility on my dad. So I didn't tell, but I didn't like the fact that he took the liberty to do that while driving me someplace. He could have done that while driving by himself. I don't remember very much about James after that, and I got my own driver's license soon thereafter.

Chapter 5

Unlocking The Code

Senior Year Finally

S O FAR, I LEARNED THE BEST OF *SELF* DIS-
covery that would prepare me well for college, and have
meaning for the rest of my life, while at the same time challenging how to handle the greatest embarrassment of my high
school years. My twelfth grade English teacher was Miss Waters.
She had a reputation for being tough, no-nonsense, I mean
strict. She was tall and thin with lanky arms and legs that seemed
to protrude, but she dressed real sharp all the time. You could
hear her heels clopping from way down the hall, seemingly a
cue to sit up straight in anticipation of the day's plans.

I was valedictorian of the class, having made the honor roll
through high school. It was my turn this day to make my oral
presentation in front of the class. Accordingly, I thought I had
prepared well, which elicited lavish praise from Miss Waters for
doing a good job, making me feel content and proud of myself.
Then while I was still standing in front of the class, all eyes still
on me, Miss Waters snapped her head to the side as she often
did in those days, wearing her dark-framed eyeglasses, and asked,

"What is an epistle?" My heart sank to the bottom of my feet. I felt stopped in my tracks as though someone had just thrown a tub of water on me. I finally said, "I don't know." She then lit into me with just as much displeasure as she had praise. Needless to say, I felt floored. I let myself down. I'd failed in my expectations of myself, but I learned that looking up every word in the title or subject of a report would help give more facts about the project. This was a valuable lesson for my future in college. I'd attended church since childhood, and I'm sure I'd heard of Paul's epistles, but I just didn't make the association from church to the classroom.

To my benefit, Miss Water's wasn't only tops in teaching content to her students, she was just as concerned about their personal out of school development, and she seemed to know everything. One morning I got to her class and went to my seat. No sooner than I had placed my feet on the floor in front of my desk, she beckoned for me to step outside into the hallway. She closed the classroom door, and I couldn't imagine what was up because this is the way she also treated students in some kind of trouble, but I didn't remember doing anything. Rolling those big eyes she began, "I know you don't know what you're doing. You don't know the trouble you could get your parents in. That house where you dropped that fellow off yesterday is a bootleg house." Well, that was news to me. I thanked her and told her that I had no idea. I had just turned sixteen and gotten my driver's license. I had never drunk alcohol. She said, "If the cops come by there and your car is there, it could be bad news." I was completely flabbergasted. I had never been in trouble with the cops. My dad's green and white Mercury flashed in my head. An aunt, his sister, lived near that street behind the school. I had visited her many times with my family but didn't know all this. I had never had a conversation with anyone about a bootleg house. Sometimes when my dad picked me up after school, someone would ask him for a ride across town. I thought this was just one block from the school, and it would be all right.

My dad allowed me to drive to school that day so that I could get home early to help on the farm. When I thought about it, for my classmate to use me in this way was the first time anything like that had ever happened to me. It was sickening. I felt angry and taken advantage of because he was older, and what I know now as *streetwise*, but still not smart enough to graduate from high school. Perhaps my English teacher talked to him also, I don't know. I had learned another lesson about the world, just naïve; how little I knew. I can't remember that happening again, and soon the class of 1958 graduated. We had a beautiful ceremony, pomp and circumstance et al., but I don't remember if I had to make remarks as valedictorian, and was very nervous if I did. Now, it was time to focus on college. I don't think the big embarrassment from Miss Water's class foreshadowed my traumatic event either, but it was an important eye-opening experience in building that part of me called *self*.

Chapter 6

Sour Grapes

To repeat, I do not think I had a com-plicated or adverse family life, and after looking back in my past from birth through twelfth grade in my quest to find a clue that could have foreshadowed my unexpected and unex-plained traumatic event, I cannot conclude any specific hap-pening that might have contributed.

However, I acknowledge experiencing love above all, and hard continuous work on our farm that taught me to complete the task no matter how long it took. I experienced fear, fun, a hurricane, humiliation, embarrassment, and even a crime, but with love, everything balanced out.

It was time to focus on college, having just graduated from twelfth grade as valedictorian, but amid all the hype, promise, and accomplishment, evil tried to sour things. My parents allowed me to go live with an aunt and work at Fort Bragg for the summer to make some extra money for college working at the officer's club as a waitress. A cousin-in-law, Robert Lee, was at my aunt's house too, but I didn't think anything of it. Robert Lee had slept upstairs in my parent's home with my brother, eaten at the same table with my family, and worked on our farm, but something sinister must have been lurking in his mind, and I don't know for how long. He tried to molest me.

In bed for the night, I unexpectedly sensed someone slowly turning the doorknob to my room. There was no knock. I didn't know who it was, but maybe my aunt was trying to get something and didn't want to wake me up. The door opened and I saw who it was. Robert Lee came in without saying anything. I was wondering if he had left something in there, but he wasted no time trying to get my panties off while I was struggling trying to keep them on. We slept in our panties growing up, which proved to be wise. Finally, completely exhausted in the fight and weighing only about ninety pounds, I started to cry. I'd never been in a fight before and had no energy left. Robert just turned and went out of the room, still without saying anything.

The next morning, I was afraid to come out of my room but relieved to find him gone when I finally ventured into the kitchen. I was wondering how I was going to face him when he came back. To my good fortune, I didn't have to. My father just appeared on the walk from seemingly out of nowhere. He had made the hour's drive to come to get me. I don't know how he knew to come, but I never told him, my mother, or anyone except my son and teenage grandson years later. They were surprised in a regular conversation that I had never been in a fight (in that fun, shooting the breeze conversation, hearing myself caused that buried memory to resurface after all those years).

I learned that my aunt had gone to New York. My parents probably didn't know she was going to leave either. I didn't see Robert Lee again until my aunt's funeral many years later. He came past me during the repast at the church and touched me to make sure I saw him. He waved and grinned widely, and then walked on. I was livid after all those years and didn't speak. There were so many people there. I'm not sure I would have seen him had he not made it his business to touch me to make sure that I saw him.

Whether or not this could be a clue foreshadowing my traumatic event, the quest of this book, I cannot say. This assault was upsetting but did not linger in my mind. The Lord must have allowed me to forget it immediately, and it did not keep me from continuing to prepare for college. I know now that this is how the Lord works. I was protected and covered by my own, and my parents' prayers. Thus, Ephesians 3:20 supports that, "He is able to do exceedingly abundantly above all that we ask or think, according to the power that worketh in us." I had never asked the Lord anything like this, but I realize now, and I'm glad to know I had such power working in me.

Chapter 7

Getting A Good College Education At NCC

M Y QUEST TO FIND A CLUE TO WHAT COULD
have foreshadowed my unexpected and unexplained
phenomenon, my *self* in shambles at age twenty-six continues.
College life greatly expanded my horizons. My parents didn't
go to college but sent all four of their children, and all four
graduated. I was very excited to join my sister Rosa, at the
historically black college then named North Carolina College
(NCC). She was a junior, and we had just spent the summer
of 1958 together with an aunt in NYC, working as nurse's
aides summer relief workers. There, I discovered I really liked
nursing, and if I had not already been accepted at NCC for
music, I would have changed my major to nursing.

On the big day, my move into the Annie Day Shephard
dormitory for freshmen women took place. I had two room-
mates, each of us having our own, separate bed. The college
experience would turn out to be the highest point in my life's
development. There was so much more to do and learn while
exploring different opportunities. I played the piano and was
a music major. However, during the first week of classes, the

first class that made the biggest impact on me was physical education (P.E.), not music.

In P.E. on the very first day of class, we exercised so hard, and I was so sore, that I could barely move without feeling excruciating pain in some part of my body. In all my years working on the farm, all the physical education in public school, and all the marching with the high school band, I had never been that sore. I was in disbelief when we had to exercise again in the next class session (despite all that soreness) but to my amazement, the soreness left that very day. The instructor said her job was to have us so fit that we'd be able to get to class on time if we woke up five minutes before class started.

Let me go back to the music department. Miss Davidson was my piano instructor. I still appreciated all kinds of music so I joined the band and continued playing the clarinet like in high school. With band and piano practice for recitals and regular lessons, I spent a lot of time in the music building associating with many other music students. All the music only helped build essentials for my important *self*. This was positive. So far, there has been no clue that I can identify which foreshadowed my *self* in shambles later. My piano teacher assigned songs from many composers, but Chopin became my favorite. I had never written notes on staff paper before but found theory class interesting as well. The instructor would give an assignment to write melodies and harmonize them. Melodies would come to me in my dreams at night. I'd get up and write them down so that I would already have one when asked.

Until this point, I'd not realized how small my hands were. With more challenging songs, I had trouble reaching an octave with my left hand, and the span beyond an octave (which I'd never tried before in public school) was problematic as well. My instructor showed me how to compensate as much as possible, but over time I began to sense that the crooked little finger on my left hand, in particular, was going to limit my future in music. I decided to consider adding French as a second major during my sophomore year. Even though I made good grades in all my music courses, my further reasoning was that I had no limitations with speaking.

So far, my freshmen year experiences continued to be positive, and nothing happened that was a clue to my quest in this book. However, before finishing my freshman year, something happened regarding dormitory life that displeased my parents. I was put off-campus. We had periodic, unannounced dorm room checks to make sure we made our beds and cleaned the room every day. As luck would have it, one day I was in the room when it was checked. There was a storage area next to our room that I'd never realized was there. The inspection lady found an empty whiskey bottle in there, and from her conversation with me, she seemed to think that I should know something about it. I never even drank alcohol, and could not tell her where the bottle came from. All I know is that I didn't put it there. I didn't think any more about this, and at the end of year, I was told I'd have to live off-campus my sophomore year. I wasn't given a reason why, but I felt it was because of the whiskey bottle. There was nothing I could do about it, and I didn't even know the name of the inspector lady. As luck would have it, my oldest sister and her husband (a veteran of the Korean War) was also a student there. They allowed me to live with them in a big house they were renting very near the campus. So it all worked out. I did not have to find housing off-campus.

In the meantime, my parents received the official letter from the college which informed them that I had been put out of the dormitory. Their displeasure showed on their faces and in their body language. I felt badly about that. To top it all off, they had allowed me to keep the car on campus and drive home the weekend before the letter came, and I got a speeding ticket. I felt like I was in the dog house. An unmarked car drove up on my bumper and I sped up trying to get away, but the car stayed on my bumper and sped up too. I was scared to stop for a white man on my bumper in an unmarked car. This was the South in the sixties, and I was a young, black woman. A myriad of perplexing thoughts raced through my mind. Then a siren and flashing lights came on and I realized it was a police car. I had never been stopped by the police before. He forced me to speed up, trying to get away, by not identifying himself as the police in the first place. After all, his unmarked car was indistinguishable from any others.

Later, my father told me that the speedometer on our car was broken and didn't show the accurate speed. This speeding ticket was a big thing. My dad had to stop work on the farm and drive me to another town to go to court for the traffic infraction. This was a very bad ending to my freshman year, but my dad never mentioned anything about this afterward. These things did not make very positive essentials for the part of me called *self*, but still contributed to the very being I was becoming.

I went back to New York City with my sister to live with my aunt again and worked a second summer as a nurse's aide summer relief worker. I continued to expand my horizons as a sophomore by pledging Delta Sigma Theta sorority and joining the NAACP back at college. I had heard about this organization as a child at my mother's church but was too young to understand that much about it. However, I knew it was to help Negroes. I also joined the college choir and sang soprano. Though I did not have a strong voice, the choir director said that being able to read music would allow me to help those around me stay on key. The added benefit of being in the choir was that we had to sing at Vesper services in the auditorium every Sunday afternoon. We sang hymns, and many I'd learned to play on the piano for Sunday school back home with my family. I also appreciated the message from the chaplain. This was a good way to help continue to feed my spiritual life because I still had a strong sense of the divine.

I did experience some challenges and disappointments with the sorority. I was called to a special meeting to determine whether I should be allowed to continue as a pledge because I didn't attend study sessions with the other pledges at the library, and missed too many of the other meetings and outings. But I was able to remain because enough sorority sisters voted to allow me to continue after I explained that my studies required spending hours practicing piano in the music building every day, and this could not be done in the library. I was concerned that I would lose the money my parents paid for this and was relieved that everything worked out all right.

Moving forward, the fascinating and smart Dr. Irene Dobbs Jackson, chairperson of the French department, came into my life and captivated my interest. She'd lived in France for several years, and had been married to a minister who had been an advisor to Dr. Martin Luther King. Dr. Jackson and her husband had several children. She also spoke French fluently. This was the age of enlightenment for me. I fell in love with French literature under the tutelage of Dr. Jackson and others. I was amazed at how much I learned. Dr. Jackson made things relevant and come alive by noting how French literature dealt with many universal themes: love, hope, suffering, sadness, joy, weakness, spiritual strength, and so on.

My most memorable assignment from Dr. Jackson proved to be quite significant in writing this book all these years later and inspired me to look back in my past to try and find a clue that foreshadowed my unexpected and unexplained traumatic event. The assignment directions were to read a novel and determine what incident, statement, or pattern of behavior pointed to a later outcome in a character's life. I always loved reading and pointed out the who, what, when, where, and had done so many times in previous studies. I had also summarized my reading often, but this was my first challenge to do this kind of exercise-related to reading a novel. I chose to apply this same exercise to this quest.

To diverge for a moment, when Dr. Jackson's son, Maynard Jackson, was elected the first black mayor of Atlanta, I felt proud to be associated with such greatness and to have studied under such an amazing woman who also helped shape my pathway in college. At the same time, I can't neglect to reemphasize Miss Waters, my senior class high school English teacher from whom I learned my most valuable lesson before going to college and meeting Dr. Jackson. The lesson I learned from Miss Water's class specifically prepared me for undergraduate and graduate study, as well as lifelong adult learning.

As expected, college was harder and more physically demanding than high school. One day I had a final French exam with Dr. Horry who was another talented professor in the French department. Before the exam, I stayed up two days and nights taking NoDoz pills to stay awake to finish a term paper. The next day, I didn't realize what mental and physical state I was in. I went to class, took my blue exam book off Dr. Horry's desk, and went to my seat to complete the test. However, trying to read the test questions, I realized that I couldn't focus, recall, understand, or analyze any of the material at all. After some time, I turned in my exam book with my name on it and walked back to the dorm. I was confused and didn't know what would happen, but realized all that mattered now, and perhaps all I could do was lie down, and so I did.

The next day, I received a telephone call from Dr. Horry. She knew I usually did my work and asked what happened. After hearing about the NoDoz and the term paper, she understood, told me to get some rest, and that we would reschedule the exam for a later time. I followed through and never took NoDoz again.

Clue

As I am writing this book on this day in November 2019, the Lord has revealed to me that the NoDoz incident is a clue that may have foreshadowed my traumatic experience years later in my young, married life. The stress of forcing myself to stay up for a couple of days and nights, while at the same time filling my system with NoDoz, caused me not to be able to think and recall the material I had learned. It was a temporary disturbance in my brain chemistry. Until this point, my system had not been subjected to anything much stronger than vitamins, and occasionally one Bufferin for pain, but nothing for two days and nights. In like manner, the incident at age twenty-six which resulted in unexpected and unexplained behavior (my *self* in shambles) was similar to the incident in Dr. Horry's French college class around age nineteen or twenty. First of all, both incidents happened over a two or three day period of no sleep. Second, in both incidents, I was putting into my system a drug I'd never taken before, and the ingredients were very different and stronger than the occasional one dose of

Bufferin before now. Third, in both incidents, my brain chemistry messed up. NoDoz caused me not to be able to recall material I'd already learned and stored in my brain. At age twenty-six, the Demerol injection I received over two or three days and nights at set intervals caused a loss of reality. This too again messed up my brain chemistry, affected my thinking, and what was stored in my brain.

I can recall the first time I experienced my brain chemistry messing up. It was after taking the medicine Excedrin. I think I had a headache and took one dose, but I don't remember if it was one or two pills. The medicine was new, just released for use, and there was glowing publicity in the news about how effective it was. I laid down after taking it, and at some point felt like I was falling through the bed. I never took another dose. I'd never experienced the sensation of falling through the bed after taking Bufferin or vitamins (the only pills I'd taken before the Excedrin). I'll write more about my theory for all this in another chapter.

Getting back to some of my non-academic college life, and still progressing in my sophomore and junior years, other opportunities meant a lot to me. As already mentioned, I wanted to ride on a float like my sister, Rosa, did in high school when she rode on the New Homemakers of America float. I was about to get that chance in college being chosen as the sweetheart by the brother fraternity to the Delta sorority. It was a huge honor I esteemed with deep humility and gratitude, but disappointment was to follow.

Rosa and I went shopping in Raleigh to find something for me to wear on the homecoming float. We found the perfect outfit after searching and walking in and out of stores. It was a gold suit, and a gorgeous pair of purple, high heel, suede shoes (these were the fraternity colors). The day of the parade arrived, and I was in high anticipation trying to wait patiently for someone to come and pick me up. The hours passed slowly. Since we didn't have cell phones back then, there was no way to find out what caused the delay. Finally, late in the afternoon, I decided no one was coming. I was very hurt and gave up waiting. All the money spent was concerning, but I kept the lovely outfit for many years. Later, I found out there was not a definite person designated from the fraternity to pick me up, but there was no time to cry over spilled milk.

I immersed myself in all my regular activities and classes just as I saw my dad do when a big load of peppers sold for fifty cents a bushel instead of five dollars. I had learned that sometimes even the best-laid plans fall through. However, there were other developments in the making. I was involved in many activities in the second semester of my junior year. I performed in music recitals and for the first time, got to go on the Northern Tour with the college choir. By this time, I think I had stopped playing with the band, but every day there was something meaningful that gave me a really good feeling. I had solid, positive experiences essential in the making of the *self* that I was becoming. Unfortunately, that *self* would be temporarily in shambles a few years after marriage, and it was not caused by anything that I'd done.

Chapter 8

The Unknown And A
Carefree Spirit (Laval)

D R. JACKSON WROTE A GLOWING LETTER OF recommendation for me to attend Laval University in Quebec, Canada during the summer of my junior year (1961). She made the compelling case that I was a good student, and could benefit greatly from studying French in the milieu in which it was spoken. I had never heard that terminology before and would never forget it. I'd visited Canada once on a short trip when living with my aunt in NYC, but to go and study for a summer would be a very rare and special opportunity. I didn't know what to expect but was pleased to learn that the work was not that difficult. Another female student from NCC and I lived together with a local family.

I remember going to a church by myself one Sunday. I didn't know anything about the church, but thinking about it now, it was probably Catholic. I just felt the spirit of the Lord was there. The service was in Latin, but just as uplifting as the services had been in my Baptist church back home with my family. I suppose I was young, oblivious, and carefree, not realizing how evil was a present reality, even amidst all the beauty. One day as an adult teacher, I was describing life in the hometown where I was brought up, and my coworker said, "You lived in a fairy tale." This may have been true because well into the summer at Laval, something happened to me that had never happened back in the states.

One bright, pleasant day, I decided to venture downtown on the city bus. It was fun strolling in and out of the different stores looking at the merchandise, and then in a flash, the sky turned darker. Hurriedly, I found my way to the bus stop to go back to the Canadian family's home where I was living. I thought, "Where did the time go?" Suddenly, a man appeared in front of me seemingly from out of nowhere. He spoke broken French and was unsavorily dressed in a dirty, torn shirt, and dirty pants. I sensed in my spirit, "Oh, no! NO! This is not good!" This unsavory man tried to talk to me at the bus stop, but I could not understand what he was saying. His broken French was a far cry from the polished and proper style I had heard in the halls of academia. The adrenalin rushed to my head, and I was breathing deeply while telling myself that I had to stay calm.

Finally, the bus came, but this character was still talking to me in broken French. The only thing that separated us was a pole that stood between the two of us. The man started pointing around the corner. All I could see around the corner was darkness, and I knew I didn't want to go around there. Perplexed, to say the least, all sorts of things flooded my reasoning. I only weighed ninety-two pounds and had never been in a fight in my life. This man didn't touch me, but he got in front of me when I tried to walk toward the bus, and he kept blocking me when I'd try to go around the pole. Everyone else who was waiting boarded the bus, and it pulled off without me.

As time passed waiting for another bus, I noticed we were under a street light. I wondered how long it would take before the next bus arrived, and a command darted across my mind, "Stay under the light." This command took me back to a sermon I'd heard from a fiery preacher when I was young and still attending church with my family in the States. The preacher expounded on Jesus, the light of the world, in his text. He proceeded to describe certain qualities of light so plainly that a young child like me could understand. The preacher explained how light would protect you, and tied it all in with his text which included references about street lights, and Jesus being the light of the world. All these years later, this sermon had a very timely message which was coming back to me and it held much more meaning now. This was God, through His unlimited power, letting me know He could protect me. I just needed to stay under the light. I focused on keeping my composure and waiting for the next bus while staying under the light. I didn't know how long it would take before another bus would come.

Time passed as we waited, and the unsavory man kept talking and pointing around the corner. Once again, the sidewalk got more and more crowded as people scattered around also waiting on the next bus. I was becoming more and more exasperated and had no idea how to get myself out of this situation. I told myself, "Never let them see you sweat." I knew I had to keep my composure. The second bus came, and the unsavory man kept speaking in broken French while pointing around the corner. He was becoming more and more agitated, and he blocked me again from getting on this second bus which also finally pulled off without me.

By now it was getting even darker. People started shuffling around on the sidewalk again while waiting for the next bus. I was highly exasperated and more confused than ever having already missed two buses. But I continued focusing on keeping my composure and trying to stay calm. The unsavory man kept talking and pointing around the corner, and then voila; a third bus came. All of a sudden I felt a hand gently ease into my left hand and an unknown man escorted me right on the bus. He led me to an empty seat and beckoned me to sit down. He sat down beside me.

I appreciated this angel sent from God. We talked, but I don't remember what we talked about other than telling each other our names. I wondered if he may have been watching for a while at the bus stop and understood the unsavory man's broken French. My French-speaking skills were still in the process of improving, and all that was too complicated for me to say in French. The bus ride was long, and when we got to where I was staying, the angelic man asked if I wanted him to get off the bus and walk with me to the door. I didn't think the unsavory character had the wherewithal to drive and follow the bus that far, and so I said, "Non, monsieur. Merci beaucoup," to the angel. I knew that God sent him to rescue me, and I now know that in the darkest hour, God is there. Romans 11:33 says, "O, the depth of the riches both of the wisdom and knowledge of God. How unsearchable are his judgments, and his ways past finding out." As the old folk used to say, "He may not come when you want him, but he'll be there right on time." And He was there. My past prayers (I couldn't pray during this situation) and my parents' prayers covered me. Now they wouldn't have to wake up back at home and read in the local newspaper, or hear on the radio, something about their daughter in Quebec.

Many times at the little country church, I'd played the hymn, "Be Not Dismayed What ere Betide, God will Take

Care of You." This proved to me at a young age that in the worst of times, God is in control. I know that no one else did it but the Lord. "His ways are past finding out." "It is no Secret What God Can Do", by Craig Stuart Hamblem. "What he's done for others, he'll do for you." That's another spiritual song I heard in my childhood. Summer school ended at Laval, and I returned to NCC for my senior year.

Chapter 9

The Sit-Ins

A
S ALREADY MENTIONED, THE SECOND
semester of my junior year (1961) was one when many things of high interest happened. Just as I was ready for college studies, I was ready to participate in my citizenship duties to help form a more perfect union, and I gladly voted when I became of age. I remembered when very young, hearing my dad tell my mom he had to go to town to pay the poll tax. My first time voting was for Senator John F. Kennedy. This was also the first time presidential candidates argued campaign issues face to face in televised debates (Nixon and Kennedy). Senator Kennedy's message had great resonance with me. He was the youngest person ever elected and seemed to have great poise. He declared a new generation of Americans had taken over the leadership of the country. I was in tune during the campaign in 1960, the inauguration on January 20, 1961, and felt he would work to form a more perfect union. During President Kennedy's time in office (about three years), Negroes made greater progress than at any time since the Civil War in the demand for equal rights.

I wasn't an angry, young, black woman and didn't consider myself an activist, but to be able to sit down and eat at the Woolworth lunch counter downtown was a worthy cause for me. It was a tiring venture to take the city bus from the college campus downtown and walk around for hours shopping, carrying all your packages, and getting hungry from all the walking, just to have no place to sit down. However, if I had known that they were going to start arresting people in Durham that day, I would not have gone down to the church to march, because I had no desire to go to jail. My eagerness to go down to the church was the news that Dr. King was going to be there, and I wanted to meet this wonderful man of God. We crammed into cars to go hear Dr. King. This was sometime in February or March of 1960, but he didn't come that day. So instead, we piled back in the cars and went on downtown.

I can't remember if I opened the car door or if someone from the outside opened it, but as soon as I put one foot out of the car and touched the curb, someone grabbed me under the arm, swooped me up, and pulled me hurriedly. I wasn't that familiar with the outside of the buildings downtown, and before I knew it, I realized that I was being ushered into the jail. This was the first day they arrested people in Durham. The jail was crowded, but I found a seat on what I think was a high bed next to a wall and fell asleep. Sometime thereafter, a person (or persons) entered the big crowded cell. They woke me up and beckoned for me to come with them along with two other girls that they picked. We were led to another area, and they said we were in contempt of court. I learned that the court was held on the floor underneath us. Others had been singing, but I was asleep and hadn't been singing. The three of us were separated and locked in different cells. I was kind of scared at first because I thought people in jail were bad. I wondered if my cellmate would try to do something to me, but I felt okay after meeting her. She was a black woman who said she was there for murder.

I didn't know what to expect. Attorney Floyd McKissick, a dedicated civil rights lawyer, activist, and veteran arrived just in time to represent us before we were put on the stand. I always smiled because my mom used to come to my bed at night and tell me to smile. Photos of me as a child often show me with a frown on my face. So when I was called to the stand and was sitting up there in that high seat, I guess I had a smile on my face. They asked me what I was smiling about, but it was just my regular facial expression. I don't remember any other questions, but there must have been. I also don't remember anything else from the whole three days and nights before being released. Attorney McKissick advised the three of us not to get arrested again because the contempt of court charge was always going to be on our records. He also told us that the trespassing charges from the hundreds of others would be dropped and taken off their records, but not our contempt of court charge. He told us they wanted to give us three girls the contempt of court charges to show what they could do. They wanted to show their power.

The philosophy of non-violence preached by Dr. King, Reverend Ralph Abernathy, and others was a way I felt that I could join the marches and protest. They urged peaceful demonstration. I already had a non-violent attitude from my upbringing by my parents. They didn't let us fight. This American racial revolution was a revolution to *get in* rather than to *overthrow*. It was a movement to allow black people to share in the American economy, educational system, and other opportunities. There were directives by the NAACP and Core Chapters, and hundreds of youthful Negroes protested to dramatize the evils of our society. Whites joined in to protest the divisive laws which governed America for too long. It was time to demand change. There was no compliance by some merchants to acknowledge change, but many voluntarily opened their places of business and charges were dropped when several other downtown stores such as Kresge and Woolworth opened their lunch counters to Negroes.

In further research, it's my understanding now that our president, Dr. Alfonso Elder (NCCU) had pressure put on him to keep the natives quiet, but he felt students and faculty were entitled to exercise their rights as citizens though in danger of having funds cut off. He brought democracy and citizenship to the campus, but at one time was told that his job was to keep students on the campus and have them study their lessons. He said, "Younger people are taking over more, and I'm all for it. I don't believe in all some are doing, but I believe in the possibilities of youth." Through his leadership, he taught a new generation of college students that freedom, justice, and equality do not come free, and must be paid for with sacrifice in school and around the community at large.

Many students started wearing Afro-American hairstyles and dashikis. An increase in relevant courses in black studies and black history was added to the general education program and selected by many students. On the national front, to meet with the growing demands of the Negroes, President Kennedy asked Congress to pass legislation requiring hotels, motels, and restaurants to admit customers regardless of race. He federalized the Alabama National Guard to enforce integration at the University of Alabama in 1962. When James Meredith tried to enroll at the University of Mississippi as the first Negro, there was much opposition, and President Kennedy ordered federal troops to restore order to the area because rioting broke out and two persons were killed on campus. I was a senior now.

The very first president I voted for, John F. Kennedy, was assassinated November 22, 1963, before the above-mentioned legislation was passed by Congress. It was my first year teaching French, and I was in my classroom when the announcement came over the public address system of the assassination. The Civil Rights Act passed July 2, 1964, and was signed by President Lyndon B. Johnson. I was very impressed with President Kennedy and the Peace Corps, "Ask not what your country can do for you, ask what you can do for your country."

It's December 2019, and Donald J. Trump is now president. I have to say, I see very few similarities between him and President Kennedy. After being in office for two years, President Trump's policies took away the annual "Good Experience" credit I usually received from my late husband's church pension. This was kind of like a bonus for keeping withdrawals at a minimum. Even though I was a widow for thirty-one years, and on disability for almost as long, President Trump's policies took my funds away, and instead increased the 401(k)'s of those who were well off. In essence, he took from me and gave mine to them, and this is how he's "Making America Great Again," and on TV he says, "Everybody is doing better. Look at your 401(k)'s" But not everyone has a 401(k). I challenge you to understand when you hear this, that he made yours possible by taking from those receiving the least…people like me.

Chapter 10

First Job: French Teacher
AND Purdue Student

I N SUMMARY, MY COLLEGE YEARS AT MY HBCU
were the most interesting time in my life because everything and everyone helped develop my career and citizenship.
However, it was a different world with seemingly mixed pur-
poses from some leaders and professionals after college. I had
always wanted to get my master's degree because I loved to
achieve, but I didn't have enough money to attend grad school
for another year. Therefore, I decided to work one year, and
save enough money to return to NCC for my master's.

In the summer of 1962, after graduating from NCC, I
excitedly received a call from the highly regarded principal of
the high school from which I graduated. He was now a principal in Gary, Indiana. He told me that he needed a French
teacher. He wasn't my principal when I graduated from high
school, but he knew my family and had been told that I wanted
a position teaching French. Like most jobs, I had to interview
for the position and had to travel to do so. This was my first
time flying, and I was very scared during the part of the trip
that required traveling on a helicopter for a connection. Seeing

all the ground underneath and everything all around made me nervous throughout the entire helicopter ride. I interviewed well (despite being nervous about the helicopter ride) and was hired. I've never been on a helicopter since and never want to again.

My HBCU prepared me very well to teach French, and soon I boarded the Trailways interstate bus to Gary in 1962. When I arrived, I was met at the bus station by Cuchie, the head of the family, where arrangements were made for me to live. His wife was a Seventh-day Adventist and had also taught school in my hometown. They had a young daughter. Cuchie's wife cooked and they made me feel very welcomed. I enjoyed sharing a room with another first-year teacher.

I attended the St. Timothy Community Church in Gary where Pastor Lowery presided every Sunday. Many other teachers attended there as well. I had no trouble getting to church because someone would pick me up, but I never joined. It was non-denominational, and Pastor Lowery called me his "watch-care" member.

At the same time, my public school supervisor for foreign language continued to allow me the opportunity to learn and grow. She visited my classroom during that first year and selected me to participate in the Summer Foreign Language Institute for French teachers at Purdue University. Teachers from all over the state attended this program, and it was a very good experience. I don't remember having to pay any tuition or housing for the twelve graduate credits that I earned that summer of 1963 at the institute. I learned a lot, and both the professors and participating teachers were wonderful. I'd never taken classes with so many white people before. One participating teacher was especially kind, always pleasant, and often sat next to me or saved me a seat. She was so nice that I decided if I ever had a little girl, that I would name her after this lovely lady, and I did, Eileen.

My French benefited a lot from the institute, and I was able to help one of my very capable high school, female students qualify for a trip to France. I then began realizing that there were so many students that couldn't read English very well, and in some libraries, there were few, if any, books about the lives of Afro-Americans. I felt I could affect a greater number of students as a librarian. Most would never use French anyway. So, I went back later to spend a year at Purdue where the twelve credits I'd already earned would count towards a master's degree in French and Library Science. However, a different story emerged from the Summer Institute for French teachers in 1963.

I took a French literature class under the chairman of the French department, but he would not call on me when I raised my hand. I'm sure the other students could see my hand up because I could see theirs. However, no one else ever said anything about how he would not recognize my hand. I was the only black person in the class. I kept raising my hand, and he kept ignoring it. He had lived in France, was married to a French woman, and had served many years in the U.S. Military in some sort of high commanding role in France. Since he was the chairperson, who was I supposed to complain to? I was not an activist, nor a Dr. Martin Luther King called by God, but class participation counted as part of the final grade. I had never been a confrontational type of person before. I loved peace and didn't want to get into this type of discussion with him about his reason for denying me the opportunity to participate in class. What I'd say wasn't going to change his reason for doing that anyway. This was the era of Alabama's Governor George Wallace who staunchly proclaimed "segregation now and forever." He also ran for president in 1968. I just wanted to get my degree and move on with my life, and get married. Therefore, I didn't dispute it when I received a B as my final grade. However, had it been a lower grade than that, I would have reported him for denying me points for class participation, because this ultimately affected my final grade.

In like manner, in one of my Library Science classes, the instructor gave me a final grade of B, but I earned an A. The Lord had already revealed to me that I needed to keep all my papers. In undergraduate school, there was a dispute about one of my grades during my freshman year, but I couldn't prove anything because I hadn't kept my papers. When I asked the library science instructor why she gave me a B instead of the A that I earned, she said, "That's what you made." I proceeded to tell and show her all the papers that I had with A's, and she said, "It must have been the final or your oral presentation before the class." I showed her all my papers and the slips I'd kept from each classmate who graded me, all of whom gave me an A. She said that she would change it to an A, and she did. This experience did not contribute to positive essentials making me the very person that I was, but I can't say if it in any way contributed to the foreshadowing of my *self* in shambles years later. I think not.

These experiences as just a regular student with the two instructors at Purdue were different from the Summer Institute where we all were teachers. I had never been denied class participation before; I was always encouraged to participate. Because of this experience, I decided that if I ever had children, I'd send them to an HBCU, and I did. All three of my children graduated with honors and got good jobs.

The French department chairperson at Purdue was far different than Dr. Jackson at NCC in regards to concern for me as a student. The difference was like night and day. I now have concerns for my grandchildren. My impression is that college is a time of being introduced to a different world which includes both good and bad attributes. Now, every time that I hear the word Purdue on TV for sports or anything, the first thing that comes to my mind is how the French literature professor and the library science instructor tried to take away from my achievement.

After completing my master's, getting rehired as a librarian was not easy even though they were adding librarians to all the elementary schools. I wanted to continue to improve and took a library science course at the branch campus of Indiana University at the Village in Gary. It was disheartening to hear the professor in that class telling the other librarians of more affluent students, how those affluent schools could qualify for the Title 1 grants that were set aside for disadvantaged children in impoverished areas. My surprise was how this great university was complicit in trying to get around federal guidelines. Perhaps, the university administration just didn't know this was happening. I concluded that these people, most of them white, want to have their cake and mine too. They make laws with loopholes that ensure that. We have a long way to go to make this a more perfect union, but I'm encouraged when I remember the spiritual song, "He Included Me," by Johnson Oatman, Jr. "When the Lord said, "whosoever, He included me."

He Included Me

I am so happy in Christ today,
That I go singing along my way;
Yes, I'm so happy to know and say,
"Jesus included me, too."
Refrain:
Jesus included me, yes, He included me,
When the Lord said, "Whosoever," He included me;
Jesus included me, yes, He included me,
When the Lord said, "Whosoever," He included me.
Gladly I read, "Whosoever may
Come to the fountain of life today";
But when I read it I always say,
"Jesus included me, too."
Ever God's Spirit is saying, "Come!"
Hear the Bride saying, "No longer roam";
But I am sure while they're calling home,
Jesus included me, too.
Freely come drink, words the soul to thrill!
Oh, with what joy they my heart do fill!
For when He said, "Whosoever will,"
Jesus included me, too.

- Johnson Oatman, Jr.

Chapter 11

Warming the Heart

THE WORDS THAT COME OUT OF YOUR MOUTH bring you to your destiny... that is a statement that I've heard preached, lectured, or I've read it someplace. And I found those words to be true. As a little girl of about four or five years old, my brother and I used to talk sometimes about what we wanted. At that young age, the people in our lives were limited. We had no television, hardly any children's books, and no pre-school, but the preacher that we saw on Sundays was our role model. We had limited association with blacks in many professions other than black teachers and doctors (Dr. Simmons, Dr. Lewis, and later, the black dentist, Dr. Merritt). I told my brother that I wanted to marry a preacher, and he said he wanted to be a "peache" (he couldn't say the word clearly). All those good things the preacher said, we held in high regard.

When Willie and I were introduced in passing at some meeting or coming from a meeting for first-year teachers in Gary, it was not love at first sight. However, the second time we met and on ensuing occasions, there was something about his eyes that began to slowly captivate me. We were teaching at the same school for a time; I taught French, and he taught fifth grade.

The story of how the relationship progressed will just touch your heart. The first time he invited me over to his place, as we sat watching television, Willie asked, "Will you slap me if I kiss you?" "Let's try it and see," I responded. He always had a serious look on his face, but those deep-seated eyes would also light up with a kind smile. Willie was a no-nonsense, sincere kind of guy who said what he meant and meant what he said most of the time. Unlike with anyone else I'd dated, I'd sometimes have to wait for what seemed like a very long time for Willie to come over, but it was for good reason, as I would learn. A devout churchgoer, he walked to a little store-front church not far from the house where he lived with three other guys who were also in their first year of teaching in Gary. There at that little store-front church, Willie had accepted the responsibility of meeting the truck driver who delivered the heating oil for the church. Though waiting for him seemed like hours sometimes, I never complained. I was just always glad when he pulled up in his blue Chevrolet Impala. I understood. As it turned out, he was doing well; it wasn't like he was making up excuses. As many months passed, talk about a life together came up. He didn't try to run a fancy line on me about how he wanted to buy me a house and this and that or would work three jobs for me. He simply said, "As long as I eat, you eat." I was cool with that honesty because my mind was already set to do as much for my husband when I married as he did for me. On our farm growing up as a child, I had already seen my mother work just as hard along beside my dad as he worked. From Bible teaching later, I learned Genesis 2:18, "And the Lord God said, 'It is not good that the man should be alone, I will make him a help meet for him.'" And Hebrews 13:4, "Marriage is honorable in all."

At some time during that first or second year teaching, we met each other's families. I had always attended church and had started attending St. Timothy Community Church in Gary, where many teachers also attended, and Pastor Lowery preached every Sunday. It was a non-denominational church, but it fed my spiritual needs. Though I never joined, the pastor referred to me as one of his watch-care members. As Willie and I kept dating, I began going with him sometimes to Shiloh Missionary Baptist Church. This was my first time worshipping in a store-front church, but I was warmly greeted by its members and enjoyed the friendliness of everyone there.

For transportation around Gary, my dad signed and transferred the title of his red and white Mercury over to me after I had been working a while. Sometimes, when I was leaving to go to school, my windshield would be cleared of snow. Perhaps someone had given Willie a ride over to do that. He got his own car soon, I believe during that first year of teaching also. Meanwhile, when my first year of teaching ended, I had not saved enough money to go back to NCC for my master's which was my goal. So, I taught a second year, after which I received a graduate assistantship in Hawaii. My intent was always to get my master's degree before getting married to be able to focus all my time on a family. I'd always wanted to travel also to Hawaii and Niagara Falls, seeing the beautiful pictures in public school textbooks and on TV. At the University, I taught a class in beginning French, and took a class in world literature, I think, to count towards my master's degree.

Willie and I kept in touch writing letters every day that first summer session in Hawaii. The only assignment I remember in that class was to read the book of Ecclesiastes. Though always a churchgoer, I'd never read that book in the Bible about a time and a place for everything. I'd never had an instructor like this before either. There were hardly any class discussions or any written assignments that I can remember. But what I do remember is the instructor came to class every day in bare feet and lectured often with his feet on the desk. The only exam or grade for anything I remember was the final, where I received a D and had no idea what it would be until receiving my transcript in the mail back on the mainland. There was no way to find out anything about the grade either. Only my second time ever receiving a D all through public school and college, this was the nail in the coffin for a master's degree in Hawaii. It would be very difficult to overcome a D starting like that.

Nevertheless, I had enjoyed all the beautiful sites in Hawaii. One tour of fifty churches was quite moving and eye-opening. The different styles of architecture of the churches were unlike anything I'd ever seen. But the message of how all of them pointed to God in their respective world cultures was similar. For example, "Rice is the staff of life," was engraved in one church which for me was saying the same thing as, "Bread is the staff of life," which I'd seen engraved and proclaimed on some church furniture like communion tables and also in sermons in the Baptist church. I saw the universality of how God provided the same for his people in different parts of the world. Touring the Polynesian Village was also a heightened learning experience, seeing how different people lived, how their homes were built, the different bedrooms and kitchens, and so on. And then one weekend, some friends invited me to an outdoor Peter, Paul, and Mary concert where they sang, "This Land is your Land," and "If I had a Hammer," really an enjoyable outing. Then nearing the end of the first summer school session, a couple from another one of the smaller islands invited me over for the weekend; again there was more natural beauty. But back in my dorm after returning from the small island, I was unnerved. It changed on every area where it landed. I had nothing to reach it with and was too scared it might jump on me. We had lizards growing up on the farm when I was young, but I didn't like them then and was scared of them back then, but never remembered one getting trapped in the house in one room running everywhere, changing colors like the one in my dorm. But it was time to go back to the mainland. That first opportunity to see many places and many things as already mentioned, and though I loved traveling, everything dazzling my eyes and the natural beauty of this place, came to an end. But as the song used to go "I left my heart in San Francisco" by Tony Bennett, my heart was in Indiana.

Still having the opportunity to return to Purdue that year, due to prior enrollment for the Foreign Language French Language Summer Institute in 1963, Willie would drive down to campus to visit me, and I'd drive to Gary some weekends to visit him. The work-study program helped make my master's degree possible. In keeping with a devout character, Willie gave me a copy of a white leather Bible that zipped closed, signed with love, and dated December 25, 1965. This gift I knew I'd always cherish and still have it. After completing the requirements for the master's degree from Purdue in May 1966, the big day for our wedding finally arrived on June 12, 1966. Pastor Lowery from St. Timothy Community Church where I was still a watch-care member performed the wedding.

Keeping the wedding in view, my mom and dad took time off from farming during this very busy season for planting crops and setting out tobacco and pepper plants in the fields.

And the two of them embarked on the long drive taking them through the scenic mountains to attend our wedding in Gary. My three other siblings were already married and all of them attended except my sister, Rosa. Willie's only brother, Arthur, also attended on his way to do his tour of duty in the army during the Vietnam War.

It was a very beautiful wedding. Friends at Willie's school planned, purchased everything, and decorated the place. Just talking with my dad at one of the gorgeous tables, I mentioned something that hadn't gone quite right, so I thought. But my dad, a soft-spoken gentleman of few words said to me, "Alice don't worry about that; this part is just for the public anyway. But the marriage is for you and Willie for the years to come." I appreciated such powerful words of wisdom. This premonition conveyed to me what was important. I felt sorry and later admonished myself for an inappropriate thought and asked God's forgiveness. These lovely ladies who had planned everything and done all this out of their love for Willie deserved only praise. We were married for twenty-two years.

Going forward, in our first or second year of marriage, Willie asked one day, "Mary, what would you do if I said I wanted to go to the seminary?" This was an omen, a signal bell. Reflecting on my upbringing, having always gone to church since birth, which led me as I grew and learned to my embrace of the Bible, I knew I'd better respond appropriately. I had high reverence for pastors. They had helped shape my life. Both Willie and I had been brought up with a reverence for God and I'm sure I affirmed this change in careers for him.

To repeat as mentioned at the beginning of this chapter, what you say out of your mouth brings you to your destiny: I had said to my brother when very young, I wanted to marry a preacher, and though I had never made that a conscious pursuit of mine, I had however asked God for a sign to help me determine if this marriage was His will for me. And I did receive the response. Proverbs 3:6 states, "In all thy ways acknowledge him and he shall direct thy path."

Just the other day writing this book, it was revealed to me the reason Willie's eyes were so captivating. The thought that eyes are the windows of the soul came to my mind out of nowhere. When my granddaughter looked it up on her phone, we found it was from Shakespeare, "Your eyes are the windows of your soul and what you give your focus, you are inviting in." In Willie's eyes was his commitment to Christ when we met. He had a relationship with God and his life proved it. And it was all in his eyes. Just because you say you believe there is a God doesn't mean you have a personal relationship with Him. Many will say that they believe in God if you ask that question. But if you ask if they have a relationship with God; this will tell you more about the person. Many believe in God but don't have a relationship with Him; never Sunday school, church, or the like of the divine. The bible says that the devil believed and trembled but the relationship between him and God changed.

As a child and on through college, Willie faithfully attended Spencer Memorial Christian Church Sunday school, eleven o'clock Sunday morning worship, Bible study with his family, his father, himself, a minister. Rev. Mack was the pastor. On Sunday evening, Willie would walk back to church, alone, to the young people's meeting called Come Double. Always dedicated to the service of the Lord, seemingly spending almost all day Sunday in church, the Bible teaches of great faith and little faith and says everybody has some; Romans 12:3 states, "...God hath dealt to every man the measure of faith." And Matthew 17:20 says, "For verily I say unto you, if ye have faith as a grain of a mustard seed, you shall say unto this mountain,

Remove, and nothing shall be impossible unto you." Willie had great faith. But God doesn't force His will on anyone. He gave us free will to make choices. Another way of saying it that I heard from a preacher is, "He makes His grace available to everyone, but everybody doesn't sign onto it."

The Bible tells us God's way for relationships: 1 Corinthians 7:14 says, "For the unbelieving husband is sanctified by the wife and the unbelieving wife is sanctified by the husband." And 2 Corinthians 6:14 says, "Be ye not unequally yoked together with unbelievers; for what fellowship hath righteousness with unrighteousness? And what communion have light with darkness?"

As time passed, I joined Willie more and more at Shiloh while we were dating and Reverend Mukes was pastor. And I joined Shiloh soon thereafter under Reverend Ward. Willie and I loved the gospel songs, singing, "I Woke Up This Morning with My Mind Stayed on Jesus," by Mavis Staples every Sunday morning at church. Also "We've come this Far by Faith," often. But Willie and I were also balanced, divine-human, and appreciated The Temptations, "I've got Sunshine on a Cloudy Day," and "My Girl", and dances too. A lot was happening in our life. One Sunday, Willie couldn't stay still in his seat, squirming, and jumped up, shouting in a loud voice, "I have to preach," in my first year attending Shiloh with him.

I learned more Bible that first year at Shiloh, with Pastor Ward preaching than in all the years combined before that going to church. When growing up, we had church two Sundays out of the month. And I still thought I was a good person and doing well if I went two Sundays a month in Gary. Reverend Ward was very knowledgeable in the Word. He had been dean of the curriculum at Hopkinsville College of the Bible in Tennessee. Hearing the scripture as Pastor phrased it, forget not to assemble yourselves together, challenged me as it often did, to look it up for myself to get the full understanding for myself. Hebrews 10: 24-25 said, "And let us consider one another to provoke unto love and to good works, not forsaking the assembling of ourselves together." I'd never heard that scripture. I just knew we went to church every Sunday with our parents.

Reverend Ward gave Willie opportunities to preach and impressed on him to study. This was at a time when many things were happening in our lives; Willie had just been appointed assistant principal, and our first child was born when the traumatic event I now call my *self* in shambles happened after a C-section, causing me to have to start psychiatric drugs, as already mentioned.

Moving right along, we soon left Shiloh and Willie became youth pastor at Park Manor Christian Church in Chicago, while also attending the Chicago Theological Seminary, both about an hour or less drive from Gary on the Dan Ryan Freeway. I learned under Reverend Ward that as soon as a child knows right from wrong, they're capable of committing to give their life to Christ. No scripture said you had to be twelve years old. And our daughter, Eileen, joined the church there at Park Manor at age four, where her dad was a youth pastor. And she was baptized there just before Willie was called to Detroit to pastor Northwestern Christian Church.

Willie and I had been brought up hearing the gospel preached and singing hymns and gospel songs in church with our parents until we left our family homes. Looking at Northwestern as my holy mission, I knew of no other institution whose purpose could make a difference and bring people together peacefully like a commitment to Jesus.

Answering the call to go to Detroit was not an easy decision on my part, but made through much prayer and self-contemplation to do the right thing. I loved my husband and I loved the Lord; I knew he had been called to preach, and the Bible called me his helpmeet. The thing that helped me in my decision on Detroit was to see it as a holy mission. For no other reason would I have agreed to this had I not been able to see it as a holy mission, taking that much of a salary cut, and leaving the home we were buying. Also, knowing that Governor George Wallace of Alabama had carried the state of Michigan (one of the few if not the only one he carried outside of the South when he ran for president of the U.S. in 1968) with his segregation today, tomorrow, and forever mentality was not a very welcoming appeal.

I didn't know what would happen, all the unfamiliar. But I knew Willie had greater faith than me, and I went on his faith. But as time passed, I needed my own faith and it developed. Willie was always about making room for the things of God. But I never thought of myself in any other role than helpmeet as the Bible called me. Willie was the one called to preach, not me. I concentrated as much as possible on the church but I knew without a doubt that caring for our children was also about making room for the things of God and that came first with me, their development, and future. I was passionate about our children. Psalm 127:3 says, "Children are an inheritance from the Lord," and Genesis 33:13, "the children are tender." We were greatly blessed to have Wilma first, and then Cookie (both very gentle natured and responsible teenagers in the church) as babysitters for Eileen, Ivan, and Benita until they were big enough to do more for themselves, and until Wilma and Cookie went away to college. Then Sister Booker helped with babysitting.

What I'll say now is I didn't know what the future held but found out like the gospel song says, "I Know who Holds Tomorrow," by Ara Stanphill. And I repeat "It is No Secret What God Can Do". "What He's done for others, he'll do for you." I'm still holding on to what I learned also in my childhood. Hebrews 13:8 states, "Jesus Christ the same yesterday, today and forever." And Malachi 3:6 says, "For I am the Lord, I change not." God cannot lie.

The years began to add up chauffeuring the children to school. Life together was very busy chauffeuring the children to school and around as well as just functioning living in the busy city with the church, my job, and everything. Being just a country girl from a close-knit, loving family, it was an adjustment to get used to the big city. Several years later, a song came out that said, "We're Blessed," by Fred Hammond. It said, "We're blessed in the city, we're blessed in the fields, we're blessed when we come and when we go." That song was the good news of the gospel and constantly lifted my spirit. My daughter sang it in her nightingale voice, prophesying in song, fulfilling the scripture; Acts 2:17 states, "And it shall come to pass in the last days…I will pour out my spirit…And your sons and daughters shall prophesy." It was so important to me for my children to have that secure, happy feeling I had when I was a child. All three children were in the junior choir and other church activities. Our mission around other believers somehow compensated for being away from the extended family, where their unconditional love always made me feel worthy of their love. That song made me feel better about being away from our extended family. But still, sometimes I'd think of the song, "Where Everybody Knows Your Name," by Gary Portnoy and Judy Hart-Angelo. "Sometimes you want to go where everybody knows your name, and they're always glad you came,". Psalm 115:15 says, "Ye are blessed of the Lord which made heaven and earth." And Jeremiah 32:27 says, "Behold I am the Lord, the God of all flesh," to me meant all flesh in the city and the fields. That song was a constant comfort when I'd think about it. You're blessed in the city. You're blessed in the fields.

I had lived in New York City and didn't think the big city was a place to raise kids. But I had also lived in Detroit as a student at Wayne State and had to leave because of a spot found on my lungs from a routine campus x-ray. After many other x-rays, it was determined they didn't think there was any adverse effect from the spot. But they could not determine what the spot was. I liked the individual homes and beautiful Detroit neighborhoods. I had decided that if I had to live in a big city, this could be my choice. What's more, Willie had given me an engagement ring at a locksmith there, where he took me and my footlocker to get it unlocked. I had lost the key to it. Sometime later, I asked why the locksmith instead of someplace like the beautiful scenes at Belle Isle and he said because he wanted to lock me up. Belle Isle was the most well known and to me the most beautiful park in Detroit.

Moving on to the ministry at Northwestern Christian Church, the first book Willie was assigned to read at the seminary was the *Courage to Be*, by Paul Tillich, and some form of this theme ran through almost every sermon Willie preached. It was appropriate to whoever was in church because no matter what your situation was, no matter what you were going through in your life, you had to have the courage to be. I still find that teaching is a much inspiring gift that strengthens me these many years later, yet today, especially as I get older.

Again, to diverge a bit, once when I was hospitalized and the nurse was taking my blood pressure at specific intervals because it kept going up, I knew I had to reach within myself to have that courage to be I'd heard Willie preach about so often until my blood pressure finally stabilized. I had a conscious feeling that God was monitoring my every heartbeat, every second because He knows your condition every second of every minute.

Back to Northwestern Christian Church, the membership grew. And there were several Sunday services and meetings a week, very much like Willie's boyhood church where he was in church almost all day on Sundays, as already mentioned. The gospel singing was especially stirring at Northwestern and gave a personal message. There was Laurita, especially talented, challenging us with a personal message singing "The Solid Rock," by Edward Mote. "In times like these, we need a savior … be very sure, your anchor holds and grips the solid rock." And Catherine King singing "I Made a Vow," with words and music by James D. Johnson, arranged by Kenneth Morris. "I made a vow to the Lord one day, I promised Him I'd go every step of the way." and Gerald Pauling singing "He's Sweet I Know," by Mahalia Jackson all moved our hearts. Then Linda and Betty singing, "A Change," by Walter Hawkins. "A change, a change has come over me." And others sang out of their hearts to the Lord.

The fervent prayers of Sarah and Pat with Sarah's echoing "Right now God, Right now Jesus," touched and helped many. I still call them sometimes to request that special prayer for my children in troubled times, so they'll hear from the saints they heard pray when they were growing up. I'm especially grateful that when Eileen had to have surgery to repair a ruptured hamstring, that happened as she was running with all the other nurses and doctors to answer a client's call at the hospital as an RN, I told Sarah, "I need you to pray that 'Right Now'

God prayer and start praying at 6 a.m. when the surgery is scheduled to start." I'm grateful she and Pat did so, as so did Wendy, and many others.

I still appreciate the love and commitment the members showed my husband, Lois, Cora, Minnie, Pastor James, Brother Reynolds, and the Godfreys. I wish I could remember all their names. Willie seldom bought anything for himself and so the church gave him clothes, outfits, and always an overcoat on anniversaries, but still some monies. They knew he wouldn't spend on himself but instead on his children. I'll never forget the time Sister Booker, Sister Singleton, Harriet, and Cora Kelly presented to me a burgundy leather-bound Bible with leather carrying straps. It's still my main read I keep close on my sofa.

Getting back to my family life responsibilities, my church life, and Detroit in general, the children continued to grow and develop as I continued taking many psychotropic meds and dealing with their side effects; at the same time helping support the ministry. We would live in Detroit for fifteen years but I had no idea we were having our last years together. But as Mohammed Ali said, "Don't count the days, make the days count," that's what we were doing anyway.

In the wonder of what was now two episodes of the loss of control of reality, I mentally revisited our four years dating and our earlier years, how sometimes life was seemingly so perfect, many days just on top of the world. And I'd suddenly catch myself and wonder what all the new happenings meant and what was down the road. I reasoned that Jesus never promised us a problem-free life, realizing that one cannot necessarily be 100 percent healthy all the time. I could see affording college for our first two children but not for Benita. Having had to stop work, I accepted the things we could not change. But I'd always believed, where there's a will there's a way.

Accordingly, I resolved to not have Benita wash dishes but free up all her time to study, hoping she'd qualify and receive a four-year college scholarship that would be awarded at the end of the eighth grade in a program my husband had found and took her to participate in on weekends for high achievers. We had ups and downs, good times and hard times, but the better times overwhelmingly outweighed the hard times. I always kept in mind the love of the first songs I'd learned to play from the Gospel Pearls for Sunday school when I was a child. "Be not dismayed what ere Betide, God will take care of you," and one of His promises that He'll never leave you or forsake you. All three children did well in school and were good children. My fervent and daily prayer was for all our children to be able to go to college and graduate as Willie and I had done, especially with me having to stop working.

The time passed quickly. Eileen studied under a gospel music teacher and learned to play gospel songs without music on the piano, and played for the junior choir. She had permission to go to the mall with Tracey who lived across the street, and others to have an outlet of independence and fun, for balance in her life. Ivan and Myron, a friend who lived across the street loved going go-carting, and Benita liked visiting her friends Monique, Trina, and Nicole.

It was time for Eileen to learn how to drive; we enrolled her in Sears Driving School. I felt riding with her would be too great a challenge with the side effects of my meds, the increased intensity of traffic, and my forgetfulness. But she already had many opportunities to drive around the country lanes on my parents' farm where we visited at every opportunity. She learned to be a good driver and was able to drive to school her senior year in high school.

Then second following Eileen, was my son's turn to learn to drive. I was quite relieved, and perhaps Willie too, that driver's education was available in the public schools by then. But Ivan had driven the tractor on the farm and the car a little too. One day, I picked him up from driving class and noticed a scratch on the left, front side mirror. I thought back and vaguely remembered getting close to a truck. Another time, a car had stopped because I had the right of way but then changed his mind and failed to continue honoring my right of way. Instead, he pulled off after he had already stopped, colliding with me and damaging the Bonneville. That was the first time I remember being in an accident when I was driving, but Willie couldn't do all the driving for the church and the family too. I told my psychiatrist I felt I should have been able to stop and avoid that collision. But I felt the meds affected my reaction time. And he cut back on my meds.

We still liked to travel but most of our travel as a family was to visit relatives in the South. My husband always liked stopping by the amusement park in Sandusky, Ohio and maybe planned to take the children anyway when we didn't make the trip to North Carolina. The children liked to ride the roller coaster but I was too afraid to get on it. Willie loved the park too. He did not take many Sundays off from the church but did have a trip to Hawaii. And the church planned a vacation for the family to Toronto, Canada when Eileen was a junior or senior in high school, and we all enjoyed it.

It was now time for Eileen to go to college and so plans were made for her to go out of state to an HBCU. There were no HBCUs in the state of Michigan that I knew of. And I didn't want her to have to experience what I experienced at the predominately white university in that part of the country in graduate school. Many of my extended family had gone to HBCUs, graduated, excelled, and got good jobs. I saw how many blacks started at predominately white universities and did not graduate for some reason or other.

As fate would have it, when it rains it pours, and the rain falls on the just and the unjust. My husband went to get diagnosed with a medical condition, was admitted from the emergency department, and kept hospitalized for four weeks. He had colon cancer that had already spread. Feeling very bad that I could not stay with him due to my condition and the need to stay with our two teenagers who were still in the home, we were very blessed when four ladies from the church took turns and kept someone with him around the clock.

The scripture Willie had the church read every week in Bible study gave me strength and took on more meaning, Isaiah 65:24 says, "And it shall come to pass that before they call, I will answer and while they are yet speaking, I will hear." It was being fulfilled by those ladies who God had prepared to do this. Six weeks from his initial visit to the emergency department, he passed away at age forty-eight. It seemed like he had prepared us for this from the Isaiah 65:24 scripture he led every week in Bible study and the exhortation to have the "courage to be" a theme in his preaching most every Sunday. He had requested "The Lord Will Make a Way Somehow," by Thomas A. Dorsey to be sung at his funeral. "The Lord will make a way somehow, when beneath the cross I bow. He will take away each sorrow ..."

My mind went back to when the two of us were waiting for our first child, Eileen's birth, and I visited him at the hospital in Chicago when they gave him a fifty-fifty chance, they could find a drug for the throat infection. We had visited many doctors for some time with no success. Tetracycline was a new drug on the market, and his infection started responding to it. And so I knew all this and was very thankful that God had already extended his life many years. I thanked the Lord too that he allowed Willie to be in our lives long enough to help the children develop their outlook on life.

When we were called to Northwestern to begin ministry there, the district church paid for our move to Detroit. Now at Willie's passing, I had no such backup to help the family move anyplace. But Minnie Givhan, another member, was moved by God to spearhead and carry out plans to make all arrangements and pay for the cost to move us. With bake sales, teas, dinners, etc., everyone had the opportunity to contribute to our move. Again the fulfillment of the scripture that, "before they call he will answer..." our reading at every Bible study meeting. God keeps his promises. Hebrews 6:10 says, "For God is not unrighteous to forget your work and labor of love, which ye have showed toward his name in that ye have ministered to the saints." That's what my husband did for many years, and I was his helpmeet. I never thought of myself more highly than I ought, and never aspired to preach, and never lost sight of who was called to preach which is not easy. But God is always right. He cannot lie. And He'll do what He says He will do. But He works on His own timetable.

Chapter 12

Head of Household

S HORTLY AFTER WILLIE'S PASSING, MY FIRST eye-opening realization impressed upon me was that I now had to do the good, the bad, and the ugly and I had to decide everything by myself. When you're faced with survival, you just do it. I heard someone say that on TV at some time. I'd have to show my family how to keep a shingle roof over their head and also a spiritual roof. My son called me from his job at MCL Cafeteria that he wanted to come home. It seems someone had talked to him inappropriately. Amid all my grief and an increased amount of psychiatric drugs to help with my grief, I knew I had only a few minutes to handle the situation on the phone. I was not a cussing person and never cussed in front of anyone. But I had to give some profound advice in a few words before he got off the phone to come home. I told him at age sixteen, "If you're going to work and make money and keep a job, sometimes you might have to take some s***," a shock for him to hear me say that word. But he stayed at work. When he came home, I told him the same thing happened to me in New York City. The nursing supervisor yelled at me in front of all the patients and everyone else in hearing distance, maybe as many as fifty people. I had put the dirty linen on the floor instead of in the linen basket. She was white and my dad had not allowed us to work on white people's farms growing up, though ours joined one. I told Ivan my first thought was the same as his, "I don't have to take this." But I rethought it, and I decided the next day to go try to talk to her. She said she had not remembered I was a summer relief worker and we did not have to go through the several weeks or months of training as required for the permanent workers. And so it all worked out.

The message to me in handling the job situation with my son was when God calls you to do something, He makes you able to do it. As my son told me years later, himself a parent, "Mom, you stepped up to the plate when Daddy passed, and continued to raise us until we were able to stand on our own two feet." I was just thankful and confident God would help me do what I had to do.

My grief had manifested itself in constant pain like I was bent over as if my back was broken. It was hard to do anything. Then one day, my sister Rosa sent me a religious pamphlet that someone gave her on a flight. The pamphlet told of a situation much like mine; 2 Corinthians 12:9 says, "My grace is sufficient for thee, for my strength is made perfect in weakness." To be reminded of that was therapeutic and I was able to feel my back straighten up and the pain left slowly.

The next thing I had to do was buy a car. The Bonneville was falling apart and we had planned to trade it in but Willie passed. The Lord had already placed in my mind to buy a life insurance policy on him several years earlier when a policy came through the mail for a premium of fewer than ten dollars a month and I sent it in. My plan now was to cash it in and pay cash for a new Escort, advertised as the best-selling car in America at that time. The insurance company said they had to investigate before paying the claim. They had to satisfy themselves that I had not bought the policy after finding that my husband had a terminal illness. They wanted information on past doctor visits but I told them Willie had not been to a doctor in five years. After much waiting and wrangling, they finally paid the claim. They could not find anything inappropriate with it after investigating.

At the Ford Motor Company, the salesman set the transaction up for financing instead of cash like I told him. He obviously didn't believe me, and he didn't want to redo everything. I had no one else to call with my husband passed away. So, I called my doctor who wrote a letter to Ford. He must have explained my medical condition and how the meds affected my thinking, recall and analyzing ability for the salesman. He had been very polite making the sale but became hostile, a complete change at having to redo everything but he did. I felt proud. It was my first time doing anything like this, and I had negotiated a new Escort for my family. A sermon I'd heard someplace whose text was "More than Enough" let me know that despite being compromised with mind-altering drugs, God had given me more than enough know-how to do the things I was going to have to do. He showed me he can take your circumstances and work them out for your good.

My son was a junior in high school when Willie passed and since it was on Thanksgiving Day, there was only one semester to find out if his credits would transfer and he'd meet the requirements to go to the twelfth grade in North Carolina and still graduate on time with his classmates in Detroit. I also had to get a place to move in time to qualify for in-state tuition for college.

All my siblings were kind, loving, compassionate, and ready to help make things work out. They were invaluable. My brother and sisters helped in the move from Detroit. I didn't trust myself with interstate driving taking that much medication. And so, Rosa came up and drove my two teenagers and me back. Though still plagued with bad sleep and forgetfulness, God helped me press on. A sermon by a young preacher, Clinton, who had just started preaching, came back to my mind, "Sometimes you just have to press your way."

We had to downsize to a smaller house with only two bedrooms, a dining room, a bathroom, and a kitchen. No longer could each child have their separate room. And my son, always the kind of person who tried to make things work, said he would sleep in the dining room, which left the two bedrooms for my youngest daughter and me. My oldest daughter was already out of the home.

After settling in Durham, Rosa attended many school functions with Ivan and Benita and meetings for college for Ivan. The year went by real fast and then we were finally in the stadium for the graduation ceremony. But I had not realized how that first year as head of household had stressed me out so much. I was so excited from the buildup of everything and glad that everything had fallen into place and worked out, I missed seeing my son march in, in his cap and gown. Instead, I was in the bathroom throwing up when he marched down the aisle. This was a good example for me of how the mind and body are connected. I had proof that for every thought, there's a physical reaction. Both great happiness and excitement, as well as disappointment, could trigger a physical reaction.

Moving right along, the first thought that had come to my mind when they told me Willie had passed was I'm going to have to teach Benita, then thirteen years old, to drive. But to my great relief, they had driver's education in high school here. She was a good student and adjusted very well, always making the honor roll and received the four-year scholarship to college for which I had prayed for in Michigan, in her eighth-grade year when I realized there wouldn't be enough money to pay for her college.

We could not find a black Christian Church near us after moving from Detroit, but I had already decided to join with Rosa at her church until we could find one because I knew a lot of the members there, from summer visits. The three of us attended that Lutheran Church not wanting to be grieving among people who didn't know us. Benita and Ivan eventually started worshipping with friends from their school. And my son said, "I need some rambunctiousness in my preaching." But I found the same Jesus I'd known in other churches.

In the meantime, new doctors had to be found. After some time, every new psychiatrist I saw began to ask in the first appointment most of the time if I felt sad or hopeless. And most of the time, my reply was no. I have always been a happy person, sometimes sad in grief, but not hopeless. Proverbs 16:20 says, "He that handleth a matter wisely shall find good: And who so trusteth in the Lord, happy is he." I've trusted in the Lord since birth.

With two teenagers still in the home, and Eileen still in college in another city, we needed more income. I responded to a Duke Medical Center ad offering a sleep study for patients with insomnia to get off their medication but they told me, I was not a good candidate for the study and did not accept me. However, I kept dreaming at night, seeing myself dressed and working, but I could not get a job though I had several interviews. Then one Sunday at church, we had a guest preacher, and I felt he was preaching right to me. A message from God saying, "You thought you couldn't do it, but you knew you had to." That was exactly how I felt, and after praying continually, I did get a job, but I was not able to learn what was needed, and it didn't work out. But I benefited from trying. My two teenagers finally got jobs and scholarships that helped in college. They went to college and used the college infirmary for health care.

My son got married and I was soon grandmother of more children. Due to the couple's separation, I helped all I could with my son's children. Being very observant and outspoken, Ivan gave me a Mother's Day tribute, "You had stepped up to the plate when Daddy passed and continued to raise us until we were able to stand on our own two feet." With the help of God, my siblings, and prayers, that's what I had tried to do. And as Ivan put it, "You remained strong enough for three kids to lean on though you were tired, and at times physically and mentally exhausted."

I'll always remember and keep that tribute. My two daughters and their children, in another city but not far away showed me too that God is good. I thank the Lord every day for his goodness and mercy of which I'm definitely not a stranger. Psalm 106:1 says, "Praise ye the Lord. O give thanks unto the Lord; for he is good, for his mercy endureth forever," and Psalm 23:6, "Surely goodness and mercy shall follow me all the days of my life." I heard a preacher preaching once who said, "See all that goodness and mercy back there behind me."

My grandchildren continued to grow and go to other churches, but I realize and pray for them as babes in Christ, who as babes need a lot of love. I've tried to speak to them in peer terminology that God takes care of babes and fools. And I've always tried to give them tender loving care, that unconditional love as I gave my children. I'm just as passionate about them as I was about my children, and maybe even more, not living with them. As they got their phones, I encouraged them in their peer language as I heard one of the teachers, Mr. Roland (who was also a minister), saying, "Don't forget to charge your spiritual battery."

At one point, I was told that my grandson was only going with me to Bible study so he could get to drive my car. But I was reminded of the ninety-year-old minister's wife at a meeting in Detroit who said, "The gospel is like paint and if you go around it, you might get some on you." You can try your best not to get wet paint on you, and you still might find that as hard as you tried to consciously avoid it, even later, you might see some on your arm or sleeve. My parents must have known that.

I tried to raise my children by the poem "Children Learn What They Live," by Dorothy Law, Ph.D.. Later, I read in the book *The Shack* by William Paul Young that raising children is like coloring a picture, you're not trying to show your superiority, but rather to facilitate the relationship that changes as the child grows. I especially tried to follow that with my grandchildren. And make them feel worthy of my unconditional love, as I always felt worthy of my parent's love growing up.

I have to say. It's that divine power and strength from the grace of God that has been running thru my system all these years. That divine get-up-and-go stimulation, the same as some get from a vitamin B-12 shot, but void of the undesirable side effects. Isaiah 40:29 reads, "He giveth power to the faint and to them that have no might he increaseth strength." That power in my system from God, from hearing gospel songs, sermons, and scripture, has quickened my spirit, not opioids, alcohol or the like. I told my grandchildren about their late grandfather's preaching, "No matter what situation you're in, you have to have the courage to be to get through it." That's what he would tell them now if he were still here.

Much direction for my life over the years, as already mentioned, came from preaching, some very creative. One Motor City-Motown preacher's sermon that I remember came from a popular song, "You Don't Have to Be a Star Baby, to Be in My Show," sung by Billy Davis Jr. in 1976. The preacher's message for the congregation was you don't have to be a star to be in God's program. I realized and also heard many scriptures that God is greater than any problem I'm going through, or anyone else's opinion. 1 John 4:4 says, "Greater is He that is in you than he that is in the world." I'm reminded of what the preacher said at my grandchildren's maternal grandmother's funeral, "Jesus is the only one qualified to evaluate her life." He's the only one who knows all anyone has been through and knows all about them. I love my grandchildren unconditionally, like my children, and want them to know as I heard at that funeral, no one other than Jesus is qualified to evaluate their lives and what they've internalized.

Chapter 13

My Theory

Y OU CAN DO WHAT YOU CAN AND GOD WILL
do what you can't has been a part of my belief for a long
time. My basic quest for writing this book still leaves me with
no definite answer to my quest. But I do know of God's infinite
knowledge and power because of what He's already done for
me and my family. Zechariah 12:1 says, "The Lord stretcheth
forth the heavens, and layeth the foundation of the earth, and
formeth the spirit of man within him." We are also fearfully
and wonderfully made. No part of us, our spirit or body, just
happened from sludge. After being under the care of several
psychiatrists over many years and taking varied meds, all of
which have worked together for my good, I've developed my
own theory of what caused my unexpected and unexplained
traumatic experience at age twenty-six. The doctors told me
the cause was unknown. But in retrospect, I've just recently
come across a small entry in my records about the first feeling
that something maybe was wrong, even before what I see now
as myself in shambles in Chapter 1.

The plug for the spirometer I used to keep my lungs clear
by blowing air into after surgery appeared to be dangling

outside of the outlet instead of being plugged in. But my mind couldn't reason that this wasn't right. On the contrary, I also remember thinking if I told the nurse some of these things, they surely wouldn't want to discharge me from the hospital thinking there was something wrong with my mind. I now know that something indeed was messing with my brain chemistry.

This distorted appearance with the plug I believe now was due to the Demerol injected at regular intervals for my pain. My brain chemistry was messing up or something was making my vision blurred and I soon went out of my head.

My new theory for all this formed at age sixty-four, after consulting an oral surgeon for a tooth extraction and asking him what drugs he was going to use for my pain. Because of past adverse reactions, I kept a list of things that had occurred after certain drugs or medical procedures. The surgeon said he wasn't going to use any of those drugs on my list. Having had three C-sections and other less serious surgical procedures over the years, this was my first time ever hearing that I might have a sensitivity to opioids. The oral surgeon further stated this sensitivity sometimes runs in families. Upon hearing all this, I went to the library and researched all the drugs on my list from which I'd had an adverse reaction, and found that all of them contained ingredients from the opioid plant. The surgeon also mentioned I was a small person and the amount of the dosage may have also been a factor. This made sense, especially thinking that now, I could have been getting the same amount as a 300-pound person. Until well into my twenties, I'd never taken more than one over-the-counter pill, Bufferin, or whatever for pain.

To repeat, because the doctors didn't know the cause of my *self* in shambles, I always had in the back of my mind, I could slip out of control of reality again, due to nothing I'd done or nothing I'd taken myself. I'd been counseled by some that if I stopped taking the meds, my condition might come back. And I had already decided I'd rather die than go out of my head again.

But in like manner, stopping Sinequan abruptly instead of cutting back little by little on the dosage and frequency when I also lost control of reality makes me remember that student in the news who stopped taking his meds at Virginia Polytechnic Institute and State University and killed all those other students and staff. This was a very scary thought for me, though I've never been a violent person or shot a gun. I didn't want that to happen with me. Rationing my Valium one time caused adverse behavior in Detroit also.

The revelation that my problem was not innate but instead came from an external force, came to my attention from a medical report in 2004 from Duke where my mental state was described as an unspecified type of schizophrenia (the first time I can remember hearing that) however my memory was faulty with the side effects of all the mind-altering drugs I was taking, and also getting older. Nevertheless, I've always believed that all things are possible with God to them that believe. I believed in the ordinary healing with medicine but also in God's supernatural power to heal. He's in control both ways.

To say it a different way, I reason that my understanding is limited but God's understanding is unlimited. As I'd heard somewhere, He's got the last word, and if you believe in Him, you've got the last word. I give many thanks to my last psychiatrist I've been seeing every three months for about seven years. She's determined I do not have schizophrenia and the onset for all this treatment was from the Demerol. The feeling that I could just slip out of control of reality has waned with time.

Having gone through the process of looking back in the past, writing this book, I now see my *self* as a separate part of the body that God made, just like my arm, and an outside force can damage both. Romans 12:4 tells me, "For as we have many members in one body, and all members have not the same office," and I Corinthians 12:18 further states, "God hath set the members every one of them in the body as it hath pleased him," and 1 Corinthians 12:26 "...whether one member suffer, all the members suffer with it," the mind and body work together. I realize I had taken for granted that my *self* was always there, functioning like my arm which I broke because I stepped incorrectly in some shoes with no strap on the back, tripped up my steps, and fell into the screen door. My arm was outstretched to break my fall. But nothing like that is so clear cut with my *self*.

All I can say now is my *self* is back for which I thank the Lord. My psychiatrist cut Perphenazine (which suppresses the brain centers that control abnormal emotions and behaviors) back from a high dose, to the smallest dose that it comes in, and gradually cut out other meds. My advice to anyone now is if something doesn't seem right and you're hospitalized, you need to report it to the nurse or your doctor because it might prevent a worse situation or crisis. My theory is that too much Demerol was building up in my system and I hadn't been sleeping for several nights before my unfortunate event. But God brought me back to my right mind and brought my *self* back at least twice. Ephesians 3:20 states, "...He is able to do exceedingly, abundantly, above all that we can ask or think according to the power that worketh in us." I am glad to have that power working in me.

We have to stay connected to maintain that power within us. You wouldn't go to the bank looking to get something out when you haven't put anything in. But God is so good; someone may be making deposits on our behalf, holding us up in prayer. He is infinite in how he works and doesn't mind our humanly finite limitations. He can take the circumstances of our life and work them out for our good. These words are some of the things I've learned from reading, listening to television preachers, my pastor, and just having an ear out for someone saying a worthwhile meaningful statement from whomever and wherever.

My regimen now of fewer drugs and decreased dosages has eliminated many of the side effects I had, brain fog, forgetting my train of thought in the middle of a sentence, better sleep with no Ambien. I can doze off naturally as I need and so much more. As the song goes, "I don't feel no ways tired," by James Cleveland. "Nobody told me the way would be easy, but I don't believe he brought me this far to leave me."

He never promised a problem-free life but he did say I'll never leave you or forsake you. Jeremiah 32:27 says, "Behold, I am the Lord, the God of all flesh, is there anything too hard for me?" He brought me my *self* back, after many years. I do not feel in the back of my mind now, that I could slip out of control like I use to feel.

In conclusion, after looking back and considering everything, I still do not have a definitive answer to my quest, but I decided similar to the great theologian, Rick Warren, a Christian pastor and author born on January 28, 1954, and founder of the Saddleback Church located in Lake Forest, California, "I would rather walk with God and not have my questions answered than have all my questions answered and not walk with God (pinterest.com).

"...For them that honour me I will honour, and they that despise me shall be lightly esteemed."
1 Samuel 2:30

"I pray not that thou shouldest take them out of the world, but that thou shouldest keep them from the evil."
John 17:15

" I will praise thee; for I am fearfully and wonderfully made ..."
Psalm 139:14

"They shall not labour in vain, Nor bring forth for trouble; For they are the seed of the blessed of the LORD, And their offspring with them."
Isaiah 65:23

"And it shall come to pass, that before they call, I will answer; And while they are yet speaking, I will hear."
Isaiah 65:24

"So shall my word be that goeth forth out of my mouth: It shall not return unto me void, But it shall accomplish that which I please, And it shall prosper in the thing whereto I sent it."
Isaiah 55:11

"Don't forget to charge your spiritual battery", (Rev. Roland, North East Baptist Church).

Addendum

Southern Family History

My Mom

MY MOM AND MY DAD WERE BOTH DIRECT descendants of slaves. My mom told me that her grandmother, Sarah Harrison Smith lived with them and was a mid-wife. She made house visits to whites and blacks alike on a horse and buggy that she drove. There was an interaction between the races, but also the Ku Klux Klan (KKK). My mom used to help her gather plants from the ditch bank and about, to load them on the horse and buggy for the women she helped. The surrey with two big wheels was used on Sunday and visiting on weekends. Great-grandma Sarah had to go to Raleigh once a year in connection with requirements for her mid-wife responsibilities. I listened in awe as my mom and Aunt Al told me at different times about her life. They also grew herbs at the edge of the yard, sage, mint, sassafras, and had different teas for different complaints. Aunt Al said she never went to a doctor until she started her first year teaching and had to get a physical for the job.

My granddaddy, Joshua Willard, had moved the family North after slavery, where he worked as a longshoreman and in a sugar refinery. Though the wages were good, when his mother's health began to fail, she wanted to return home. And so he returned South with his wife, three children (one of which was my mom), and his mother. There, he provided a home for his mother, Sarah, until her death at eighty plus years. Other siblings in the North sent things to help the family after the move back to the South.

It made me sad when Aunt Al told me about Sarah Harrison Smith's father Pete, who was a slave and ran away. As the story goes, Pete was called an uppity slave and his slave owner and others were going to gang up and whip him but the trap was foiled and didn't succeed. He came up with a knife and outsmarted their plan and got away from them.

Sarah Harrison Smith's mother would put out a plate of food in the woods and he'd come by and get it. So they figured he was living in the woods somewhere in the area. They put out the plate every day, but then one night, he just didn't come again to get the plate of food.

Having taken a medication that suppresses abnormal emotions for many years, I'm sure I'd heard the story before and I'd read about slaves, but this time, it was my family and it made a difference with my having been cut back on my Perphenazine, not suppressing my brain center's abnormal emotions anymore. And I wanted to cry, I felt so bad about it that he didn't come again to get the plate, and I had all kinds of thoughts of what may have happened to him, my great-great granddaddy.

It is said that he might have escaped to Canada. The United States should apologize for slavery if they haven't already. My Aunt Al, now ninety-three years old, gave me a little encouragement telling me about her trip to Canada in retirement where she saw the place where slaves had gone; as Harriet Tubman advised staying in the forest in the day and following the North Star showing the way to Canada at night.

My Dad

My dad's father, Lewis Henry, and his siblings were the direct descendants of slaves too. We got our last name from those ancestors who came to America from Scotland around 1745-1770 and eleven slaves were left to this slave owner of a small plantation. One of the eleven slaves on this small farm or plantation was Easter, the mother of six males, one of which was my grandfather, Lewis Henry. As the story is told, my grandfather and his brothers received five acres of land at the end of slavery, which allowed them to own their farms and be farmers. They also hired themselves out, built houses and other buildings, and did carpentry. That's how they made their money. My grandfather, Lewis Henry, cut the trees to build the house for his family at the end of slavery and finished around 1790, and that house is where I was born. The family church, Andrews Chapel Baptist Church, was founded and built by my grandfather, Lewis Henry, and others. My dad was a deacon there for thirty years.

After the Civil War, very few slaves owned property or made wills, so, much of what we know about our ancestors has been passed down orally from one generation to the next.

It's almost impossible for blacks to trace their roots back to Africa. The only records kept on the slaves were the bills of sale from slave ships to plantation owners or buyers of slaves. However, there are some available records.

Afterword

I LOVE MUSIC, AND I HAVE A FEW SONGS THAT I want to share with my grandchildren, and with you. Marvin Sapp wrote a gospel song entitled, "The Best in Me." The song lets the listener know that Jesus sees the best in us when other people only see the worst. This is encouraging for all of us because people often only remember and bring up what we've done wrong. I want my grandchildren to know that despite this, your Granny Watkins has always tried to make you feel special and valuable. I've always seen the best in you.

Anthony Brown and Group Therapy also have a gospel song, "Worth," that I want you to remember and internalize. The lyrics of the song share the message better than I can. The song lets us know that Jesus thinks we are valuable, important, worth keeping, and worth saving. He loved us so much, He sacrificed His own life so that we can be clean, free, and whole. Hallelujah!

I wish that I could give the talented India Arie's *Worthy* (CD) to all my grandchildren. It includes a short, four-minute glimpse into some black history in her song "What If." She uses this song to mention civil rights leaders such as Dr. Martin Luther King, Malcolm X, and Rosa Parks; artists, poets, and modern-day champions such as Serena, Oprah, Kamala, and others who changed and are still helping to change the world.

In this song, she says that every one of us is worthy. My parents taught me that and helped me feel special and worthy, and you are worthy too. When something is not right or doesn't feel right, we need you to use your voice and say something. James Baldwin wrote in his book, *I Am Not Your Negro*, "Not everything that is faced can be changed. But nothing can be changed until it is faced." You *are* the voice of change that the world has been waiting for. Speak up.

Acknowledgments

I AM DEEPLY GRATEFUL TO ALL WHO HAVE helped me with this book. Family always comes first. I wish to first thank my twenty-one-year-old grandson for bringing me good luck to get this started. I remember you at two years old standing at the end of my walk with that genuine smile from ear to ear every morning looking up at my front door, and then walking around the house telling me, "Granny, I love you," over fifty times a day. I actually counted them one day and stopped at fifty.

At the end of 2018, I was stirred in my spirit to ask him if he would come over to my house on New Year's Day and be the first one over and walk through my house. This was a practice from slavery, in the African culture; that the first male to come over and walk through your house the first day of the year would bring you good luck for the rest of the year. He said he had never heard that but said he'd come. Late in the morning, January 1, 2019, I waited, wondering as the time passed if he was going to wake up and make it. Then at 11:30 a.m., I heard his footsteps on the porch. He came in and said with anticipation, "Granny did I make it?" and I said, "Yes, grandson, you made it. And you have brought me good luck." I could feel in my spirit something was going to happen. Then in two days, on January 3, 2019, I had an appointment with my psychiatrist who I'd seen for the last seven years. I could hardly get in her office to say hello before she said, "You don't have schizophrenia." She cut my meds way back eventually, but gradually to two milligrams of Perphenazine and decreased all the others. I'd been taking psychotropic meds in varying dosages some fifty years. After waiting several months with better sleep without taking Ambien every night, and without feeling I was going to slip out of control of reality, and having more energy, a better memory, a clearer mind, and clearer thinking, and analyzing better, I decided to write this book. My doctor had already started cutting my meds back about a year before, but it was not until now that I felt ready to start the big decrease because of fear of the condition possibly coming back as I had been told by a few doctors. My doctor had been sent by God to be my doctor and I am thankful.

A second thank you goes to Aleah, my eighteen-year-old granddaughter who always showed love and was ready to look up something on her phone (before I bought my thesaurus) including Googling since I'm not in the twenty-first century yet with technological gadgets and not tech-savvy. She helped in many other ways too.

To my late parents and my late sister, Rosa; I want to thank you for anchoring me in a can-do attitude, my parents always telling their children you can do anything you set your mind to do. Thank you, Aunt Al, age ninety-two, a senior English teacher for many, many years, who listened to my first few paragraphs and encouraged me, she wanted to read my book in her lifetime. She also shared southern family history. I'm deeply grateful to Joe, my brother-in-law who was in college in the French department at the same time as me. And thank you to my brother, Sam, my first playmate, and then attending all public schools together and for giving invaluable farm information and farm history.

This book would not have been possible without my oldest daughter, Eileen, who did the lion's share of typing from my cursive drafts and typing my edits; how much you mattered! And to my youngest daughter, Benita, thank you for your internet ability to get information on publishing, etc., and just that ready love, an ear, and a phone call at good timing. Thank you also to my son, Ivan, for the pictures and other help; for always being there. And to my first cousin, Sammie Edward, for pictures and family history; and Linda Rich Lyons for the picture from my class of 58 high school reunion.

There are so many others I wish to thank: Mrs. Heartwell, Walter Weathers, and Ms. Terry before I found a typist who could commit. Thank you to my friend Juanita with info about questions for agents. Thanks also goes to Wendy Reynolds who passed away, Shatira, Dr. Monroe, Bill Evans for connecting me with phone calls with the archives librarian at NCCU, and Mrs. Caldwell, retired home economics teacher. To my homegirl, Brenda, who I met in the eighth grade, and went to the same college together, thank you. A big thanks also goes to Majoice, Ms. Kim, and Carol. I also have to thank my grandchildren: Askia, Amory, Amerie, and BJ. And thanks to Camryn and Caden who made me have a delightful stay in their home; Camryn for giving up her bed and Caden bringing in my suitcase, and all their "Hi Granny's" passing in the hall throughout my stay to collaborate with my typist and editing, just delighting me with their love.

Thank you to Sister Babs and my niece, Debbie, for being the only ones who could keep Aleah, my first granddaughter from crying to relieve me during the time I was keeping her as a baby years ago. And now Aleah is contributing so much to this book.

And thanks to Porsha, a good friend from the (Millennial Generation). Thank you, Mrs. Blake, a good neighbor and friend for sharing an inspiring book about grace when I lost a good friend of thirty years which moved me out of a period of writer's block near the end of my writing.

And thank you, Carl, the good neighbor who's like a son and comes through in a pinch for Fed Ex copies and whatever I may need. I would also like to thank my sister-in-law, Sadie Edwards, for valuable information on my husband Willie while they were growing up. And I thank Rev. Darryl Williams and Betty Gwynn.

Lastly, a thank you to Walter Weathers, there from the beginning when no one else could commit and during the end of production, I say thank you a thousand times. I say thank you to all of you.

I hope that this book, part memoir, and inspirational, shows how the different scriptures and gospel songs helped me press on until my change came, which I believe was God's unlimited, supernatural power that brought my *self* back.

"The Lord
will
guard
your
going
Out and
your
Coming in
From
this
time
forth
and
forever."
Psalm 121:8 (NASB)

Abbreviations

(NASB) New American Standard Bible
(KJV) The Holy Bible King James Version
(PDR) The Physician's Desk Reference

Notes

Chapter 2: Pressing Forward

Valium (PDR).
Halcion (PDR).
Restoril (PDR).
Ambien (PDR).
Demerol (PDR).
Codeine (PDR).
Sinequan (PDR).
Stelazine (PDR).
Cogentin (PDR).
Temezepam (PDR).
Haldol (PDR).
Amitriptyline (PDR).
Levoxyl (PDR).
Perphenazine (PDR).
Fentanyl (PDR).
Romazicon (PDR).
Narcan (PDR).
Dilaudid (PDR).

Chapter 4: Up and Becoming

Category-4-Hurricane-North-Carolina-Hazel, http://www. history.com/news/.

Hurricane Hazel, https://en.wikipedia.org/wiki/.

Chapter 9: The Sit-Ins

North Carolina Central University Archives. Non-violent teaching for demonstrations at lunch counters came from the NAACP and Core leaders. Dr. Martin Luther King, Reverend Ralph Abernathy, Attorney Floyd McKissick (a dedicated civil rights lawyer).

The World Book Encyclopedia. Volume 11, J-K. "United States: Field Enterprises Educational Corporation, 1973." President John F. Kennedy asked Congress for legislation demanding changes for Negroes but was assassinated November 22, 1963.

CPSIA information can be obtained
at www.ICGtesting.com
Printed in the USA
LVHW071447220921
698454LV00001B/6